Published by

krause publications
700 East State Street • Iola, WI 54990-0001
715/445-2214 • FAX: 715/445-4087   www.krause.com

Please call or write for our free catalog of publications. Our toll-free number to place an order or obtain a free catalog is 800-258-0929 or please use our regular business telephone 715-445-2214.

Library of Congress Catalog Number 2001092238
ISBN 0-87349-366-4

Note: The Original Be-Dazzler Stud and Rhinestone Setting Machine is intended for adult use.

Introduction

Over the years, fashion trends come and go, but there is almost always a resurgence years later. In the 1970s, during the disco era, glitz and glam were staples in the wardrobes of men and women alike. And who can forget the "punk look" popular in the 1980s? Dog collars, belts, and jean jackets covered with spikes and studs were seen on both everyday people and celebrities. Today, people of all walks of life are wearing clothes and accessories adorned with sparkles, studs, and rhinestones—some of which cost hundreds of dollars! That's why the Be-Dazzler Stud and Rhinestone Setting Machine is back!

This unique compilation is filled with more than fifty fashions, accessories, and home décor items, all of which can be embellished with studs and rhinestones. While this book includes detailed instructions, and even patterns, let it be a springboard for creativity; for instance, if you don't like an aspect of a project, change the number, size, or type of stud or rhinestone shown to make it uniquely yours! And, as an added bonus, we have included information for adding various trims and even wire beads to your designs, so your creations will have even more flair.

Finally, visit www.nsiinnovations.com, NSI Innovations' website, for more information on the Be-Dazzler machine and the company's other products.

Have Fun and Be Creative!

Table of Contents

Be-Dazzler
Supplies and Basic Techniques 6

Wild Wire
Supplies and Basic Techniques 14

Section 1
Projects for You 20

Section 2
Projects for Your Home 54

Patterns 78
Project Index 93

Multi-colored rhinestones.

Be-Dazzler
Supplies and Basic Techniques

Before starting any of the projects in this book, take some time to review the information on the following pages; not only will you be amazed by the awesome variety of studs, rhinestones, and other trims that you can use to embellish clothing, accessories, and home décor, but you will also get a crash course on the proper way to use the Be-Dazzler Stud and Rhinestone Setting Machine and other tools, which will come in handy, even if you have used them before.

Cool Coordinates.

Be-Dazzler Machine.

Supplies

The Be-Dazzler Machine safely and accurately sets studs into fabric. It adjusts easily to fit the round studs in the Be-Dazzler range and can also set rhinestones with a tiffany setting. The Stud Insertion Tool is a must! This tool is included in the Be-Dazzler Stud and Rhinestone Setting Machine Set. This tool safely inserts studs and settings into the Be-Dazzler machine, without your fingers having to press down on the sharp points of the prongs.

Be-Dazzler gold- and silver-colored studs come in many different sizes and shapes. Each stud has a decorative front with sharp prongs on the back to secure the stud to the fabric. Colorful rhinestones can also be attached to fabric. A tiffany style setting with prongs is required to set rhinestones.

The Be-Dazzler Hand Tool sets very large or unusually shaped studs, including hearts, horseshoes, and peace signs, into fabric.

Be-Dazzler Cool Coordinates sets contain appliqués, as well as decorative trim and studs, to further embellish your fashions. These appliqués can be attached with a hot iron or fabric glue.

A vanishing or washable fabric marker is ideal for marking designs onto your fabric, if you are not using a pattern. With this pen or marker, you can accurately plan out your design, and the markings will either fade or wash out. If you are not going to mark designs on your projects "freehand," you can trace any of the full-size patterns included in this book onto tracing paper, and then transfer them to your fashions with a hot-iron transfer pencil.

A sampling of studs.

Custom Hand Tool.

Techniques

While we know you are anxious to get started creating cool fashions, accessories, and décor for your home, the following step-by-step instructions will help ensure success!

▾▴◂▴◂▴◂▴◂▴◂ Directions for Using the Be-Dazzler Machine ▴▾◂▴◂▴◂▴◂▴◂▴◂

The Be-Dazzler machine can set #20, #34, #40, and #60 round studs and rhinestones. This includes all flathead studs, round diamond cut studs, pearl studs, ringlets, mirrors, small flowers, small stars, and happy face studs. Two parts of the Be-Dazzler machine have to be changed each time you set a new size stud: the plunger and the setter plate.

▾◂▴◂▴◂▴◂▴◂▴◂▴◂▴◂ Changing the Plunger ◂▴◂▴◂▴◂▴◂▴◂▴◂▴◂

The Be-Dazzler machine comes with four different size plungers. Choose the plunger that matches the size of the stud or rhinestone you are setting (for example, a #20 plunger would be used to set #20 studs).

1 To insert the correct size plunger, lift the arm of the Be-Dazzler and slide the plunger holder down and out of the arm.

2 Pull apart the two halves of the plunger holder and remove the plunger. To insert another plunger, fit one tab at the top of the plunger into the notch on one half of the plunger holder. Close the two halves of the holder.

3 To slide the plunger holder back into the arm of the machine, fit the long tab along one side of the holder into the long groove inside the opening of the arm.

▾◂▴◂▴◂▴◂▴◂▴◂▴◂ Adjusting the Setter Plate ◂▴◂▴◂▴◂▴◂▴◂▴◂

The setter plate, located on the base of the machine, has four settings. **Note:** If the setter plate does not turn easily, the plate can be adjusted. Use a Phillips screwdriver to loosen the screw at the center of the plate. Turn the wing nut (located at the other end of the screw, under the machine) as you loosen or tighten the screw.

1 Rotate the setter plate according to the size of your stud. If you are setting a #20 stud, for example, turn the setter plate so that the tip of the plunger aims directly down into the center of the #20 setting.

> The #20 setting sets both #20 and #60 studs and rhinestones
> The #30 setting sets #30 studs and rhinestones
> The #34 setting sets #34 studs and rhinestones
> The #40 setting sets #40 studs and rhinestones

Always use the insertion tool to insert studs into the Be-Dazzler machine! The sides of the tool correspond to the different size studs or rhinestone settings. There are two types of tips for each size: a flat tip and a pointed tip. Use the flat tip for studs and the pointed tip for rhinestone tiffany settings.

1 To set a stud, slip a #60 stud over the #60, for example, onto the flat tip of the tool. With the stud held in place on the insertion tool, push the stud securely into the tip of the plunger.

2 Place your fabric, right side up, over the setter plate on the machine. Lower the arm of the machine, checking for accurate placement of the stud, then press firmly on the arm to set the stud into the fabric.

3 After each stud is inserted, check the back of the fabric. Each prong of the stud should be bent in toward the center. All of the prongs should lie flat against the fabric and not stick out. If any prongs do stick out, use the tip of the insertion tool or the Custom Hand Tool to flatten the prong. If the prongs are facing the wrong direction, the setter plate is probably not centered under the plunger tip; also, make sure to use the correct setter plate.

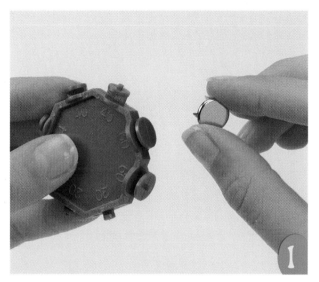

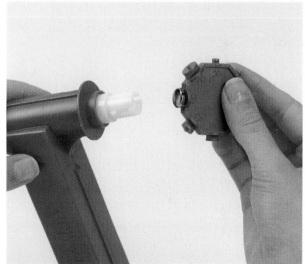

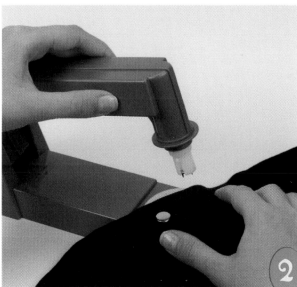

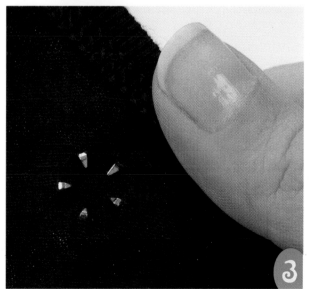

As was mentioned previously, you will use the pointed side of the insertion tool to set rhinestones onto your project.

1 Rhinestones are held onto the fabric with a tiffany setting. Slip a tiffany setting onto the pointed tip of the insertion tool. Use the insertion tool to push the setting into the plunger in the arm of the machine.

2 Place a rhinestone upside down in the setter plate.

3 Place your fabric right side down over the set-ter plate. (**Note:** When setting rhinestones, it might be helpful to mark your design on the wrong side of the fabric). Lower the arm of the machine, checking for accurate placement, then press firmly on the arm to insert the tiffany setting. If inserted correctly, the prongs of the setting will go through to the front of the fabric and bend securely around the rhinestone.

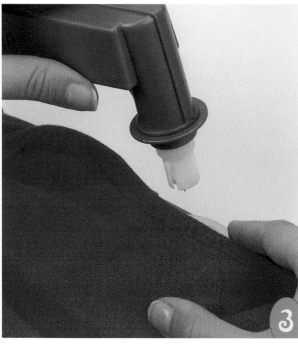

Directions for Using the Be-Dazzler Custom Hand Tool

Very large or unusually shaped studs can be inserted into fabric with the Custom Hand Tool.

1 Position the stud on the right side of the fabric. With your fingers, carefully press the stud's prongs through the fabric.

2 Turn the fabric to the back and check that each prong came through the fabric all the way. You may need to press the fabric around each

prong to assure a tight fit. Avoid touching the tips of the prongs.

3 Slip one prong of the stud inside the small slit on the hand tool. Use the hand tool to bend the prong in toward the center. Once all of the prongs are bent in toward the center, use the raised rounded area of the tool to press them flat against the fabric.

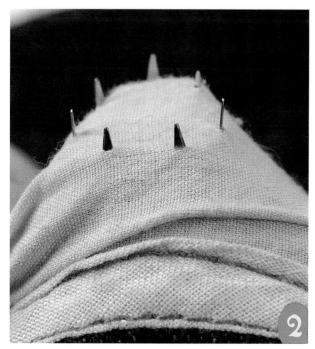

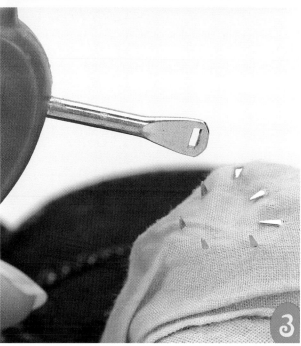

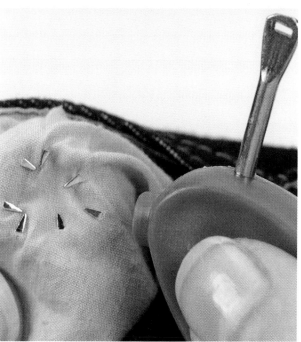

While embellishing fashions, accessories, and home décor with only studs and rhinestones may suit some people, for others, the more embellishment the better! Now you can add funky fringe, ribbon, and a variety of appliqués to your creations with an iron or fabric glue—and a little imagination.

1 Appliqués, like butterflies and ladybugs, can be applied to your project will an iron (follow the Cool Coordinates package instructions). (**Note:** You can also glue appliqués to fabric, as shown.)

2 To apply fringe and ribbon to a project, use fabric glue, as shown, following the manufacturers instructions. First, apply the fringe, all around the edge of the project. When the glue is completely dry, attach ribbon over the fabric edge of the fringe with fabric glue. The ribbon ends should overlap in an unnoticeable place on your project, like an inner seam. Turn the overlapping end under as you glue it down to prevent the edge from fraying.

You have two options for completing a project: "winging it," by placing studs, rhinestones, and trims based on your liking, or by using the full-size patterns included on pages 80 through 92 in this book. Transferring patterns is not terribly difficult, but you need to be patient and cautious, because you don't want to ruin your project with a skewed or misplaced pattern.

To transfer a pattern onto a project, you will need a few miscellaneous tools: a hot-iron transfer pencil, tracing paper, a ruler, vanishing fabric marker, an iron, and your chosen pattern. **Note:** Always test the hot-iron transfer pencil and vanishing fabric marker on an unnoticeable area of your project and follow all manufacturer instructions to ensure satisfactory results.

1 Trace the pattern onto the tracing paper using the hot-iron transfer pencil.

2 If you want your pattern placed at the center of your project, fold the fabric in half; mark this place with the vanishing fabric marker.

3 You can also use the vanishing fabric marker and a ruler to draw a line that will denote where you want the top of the pattern to begin.

4 Place the tracing paper face down onto the project, lining up the top of the pattern with the line drawn in Step 3 and keeping the middle of the pattern in line with the mark from Step 2.

5 To transfer the image to your project, press a hot iron on the tracing paper for about 60 seconds. Note that this design is permanent, so take care when setting your studs and rhinestones!

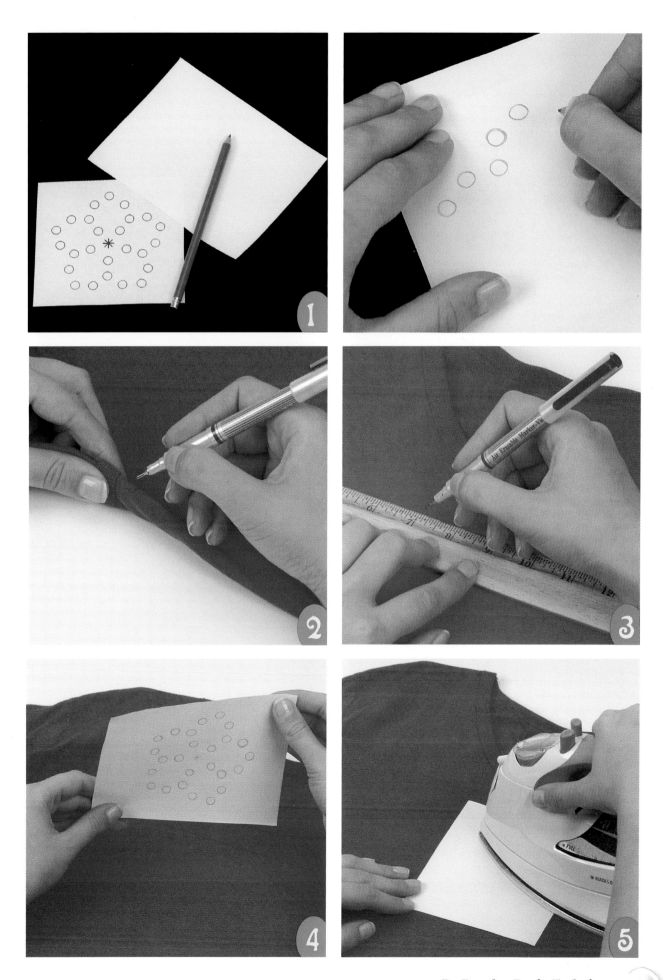

Wild Wire

Supplies and Basic Techniques

A sampling of wire.

While the focus of this book is on the Be-Dazzler machine, the addition of Wild Wire to a project can add a feel of whimsy, as shown on the pillow on page 68 or the tablecloth on page 76.

This section gives you the basic information about supplies and techniques you will need to embellish any project shown in this book.

Supplies

Craft wire is available in various colors and gauges. The higher the gauge number, the thinner the wire. All of the projects in this book utilize wire that is either 20 or 22 gauge, but practice with a few different gauges and see which works best for you and your particular project.

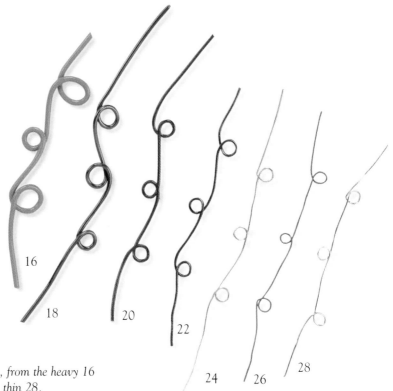

16
18
20
22
24 26 28

Wire in various gauges, from the heavy 16 gauge to the thin 28.

▾◂▴▾◂▴▾◂▴▾◂▴▾◂▴▾ Pliers ◂▴▾◂▴▾◂▴▾◂▴▾◂▴▾

Round Nose Pliers are the most basic tool in wire craft. The nose of these pliers is made up of two tapered round metal tips that grasp and bend the wire. As you squeeze the handles together, you close the gap between the tips of the nose. Many round nose pliers also have a wire cutter, found just under the nose. To use the wire cutter, spread the handles open and slip the wire inside the cutter. Squeeze the handles together to cut the wire.

Flat Nose Pliers have angular tips. This type of pliers can be used to create sharp angles in the wire as well as to grip and bend it.

Bent Chain Nose Pliers allow you to grasp and manipulate wire a little more easily, especially with smaller, more intricate areas.

Nylon Jaw Pliers are great for smoothing out wire. If the wire you are using gets bends or kinks in it, place the bent part between the pliers jaws and press down to straighten it out. Because of the nylon coating, the pliers will not scratch or damage the wire. Flatten the wire to give added strength to finished pieces.

Round Nose Pliers.

Flat Nose Pliers.

Bent Chain Nose Pliers.

Nylon Jaw Pliers.

▾◂▴▾ Miscellaneous Tools and Supplies ▾◂▴▾

Files are used to smooth out the tip of wire if it is sharp.

A Nylon Hammer will gently flatten areas in your design. Hitting the wire harder will give the wire a unique look.

Besides just cutting wire, Wire Cutters help you snip wire in areas that may be hard to reach. They will enable you to trim off small ends that would not otherwise fit inside of your regular pliers. When cutting, always aim the wire away from your face and other people! When cutting a small piece of wire, hold the wire in an enclosed area such as a trash bin. It is always recommended to wear safety goggles when cutting wire.

Files.

Nylon Hammer.

Wire Cutters.

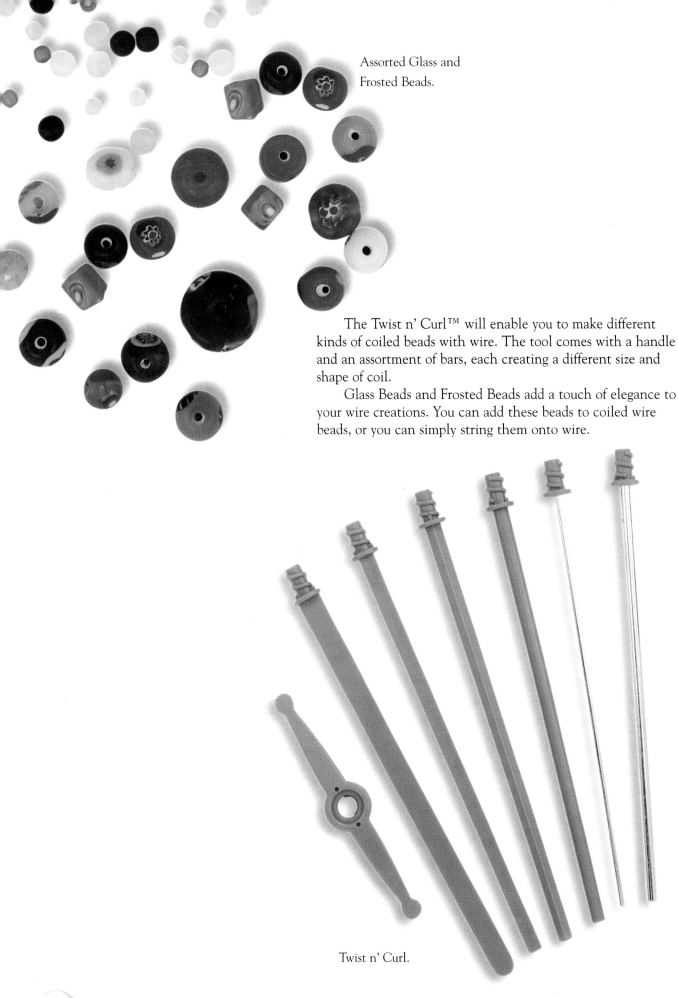

Assorted Glass and
Frosted Beads.

The Twist n' Curl™ will enable you to make different
kinds of coiled beads with wire. The tool comes with a handle
and an assortment of bars, each creating a different size and
shape of coil.

Glass Beads and Frosted Beads add a touch of elegance to
your wire creations. You can add these beads to coiled wire
beads, or you can simply string them onto wire.

Twist n' Curl.

Techniques

Using the Twist n' Curl

Using the Twist n' Curl to create single and double coil beads is quite easy once you get the hang of it. Unless otherwise noted, use the wire as it comes on the spool. Once your design is complete, you can then cut off the excess.

Making Single Coil Beads

1 Screw a bar of any shape or size desired into the hole at the center of the handle.

2 Insert 2" of the end of wire into the wire hole in the handle. Bend the 2" piece of wire so it is flat against the handle.

3 Hold the wire in one hand. As you twist the handle with your other hand, the wire will coil around the bar. Once you have created a coil of the desired length, cut off the excess wire and slip the coil off of the tool.

4 Cut off the excess wire at the beginning of the coil. With pliers, carefully bend the ends of the wire so that they will lie flat with the rest of the coil (the wire is very sharp!).

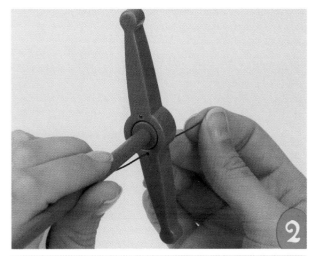

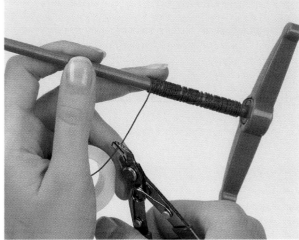

1 Create a single coil bead as directed on page 17 that is at least 3" long, leaving a 2" piece of straight wire at one end of the coil. Remove the bar.

2 Insert a new piece of wire through the center of the single coil. Attach the end of the new wire into the wire hole in the handle.

3 Wrap the new wire around the bar, creating a new coil.

4 Slide the single coil up to the wrapped wire on the bar. Insert the 2" end of this wire into the hole in the handle.

5 Hold the coil against the bar. As you twist the handle, the single coil will wrap a second time around the bar.

6 At the end of the double coil, wrap more of the straight wire around the bar again. Cut off the excess wire at both ends of the bead and remove from the bar.

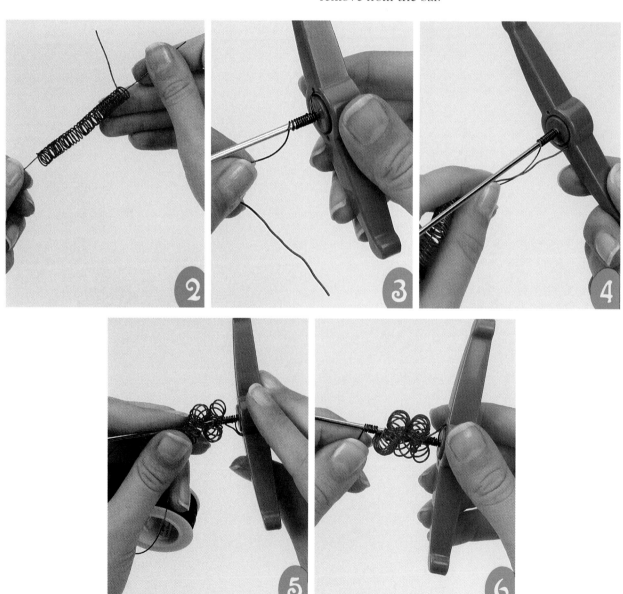

This loop will allow you to attach wire to your project.

1 Grip an end of wire between the nose of the round nose pliers. The wire should be positioned about 1/4" down from the tip of the nose. Squeeze the handles of the pliers and keep a tight grip on the wire.

2 Carefully wind the wire around the nose of the pliers one turn, creating a tight loop. This can be done by either turning the pliers or by pulling the wire around. Pull the loop off the nose of the pliers, then place the looped end between the tips of the pliers and squeeze to flatten out the end.

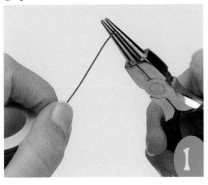 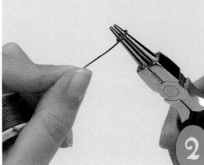 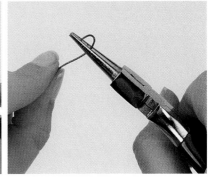

Creating a spiral is really quite easy, and it is the perfect finishing touch to any wire bead you create.

1 Make a basic loop as shown above.

2 Grip the loop between the jaws of the nylon jaw pliers. Begin to circle around the loop.

3 Shift the position of the loop as you circle the wire around.

4 Insert the end of the spiral through a wire bead or slip glass or frosted beads onto it.

5 Now create a loop as shown above and clip the end.

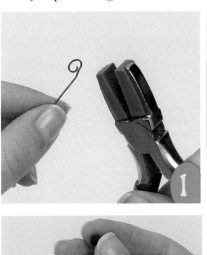 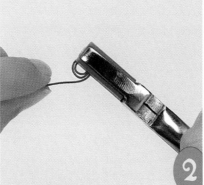 

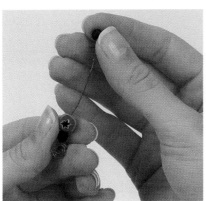  

Section 1
Projects for You

Flip through any current fashion or lifestyle magazine, and we guarantee that you will see actors, models, and rock stars dressed in jeans, jackets, and accessories that are covered with studs and rhinestones. If you don't have hundreds of dollars to buy the clothes you see on such celebrities as Cameron Diaz and Britney Spears, you can do it yourself! Short on time? Jazz up any outfit with a studded belt from page 44. Have an old pair of jeans that needs revitalizing? We've included many styles to choose from! The bottom line? Regardless of your taste or the size of your pocketbook, you can create looks that are perfect for everyday wear or for a night on the town.
Please note: The actual amount of studs and rhinestones used for each project may vary depending upon the size of your garment!

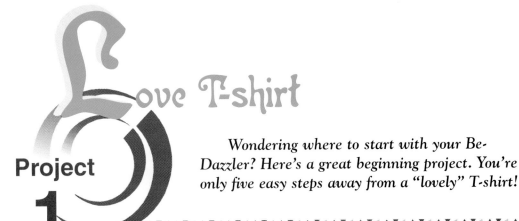

Love T-shirt

Project 1

Wondering where to start with your Be-Dazzler? Here's a great beginning project. You're only five easy steps away from a "lovely" T-shirt!

▲▼◄▲▼◄▲▼◄▲▼◄▲▼◄▲▼◄▲▼◄▲▼◄▲▼◄▲▼◄▲▼◄▲▼◄▲▼◄▲▼◄▲▼◄

Designed by Elaine Schmidt

You Will Need

- T-shirt, black
- Love pattern
- 48 #20 gold flathead studs
- Vanishing fabric marker
- Ruler

1 Find the center of the T-shirt by folding it in half. Mark the centerline with the vanishing fabric marker, as shown on page 13.

2 Open the shirt again and lay it flat on your work surface.

3 Decide how far down from the neckline you would like the design to go. Using the ruler and vanishing fabric marker, draw a line, indicating the top of your design. (Check that your line is straight by measuring the same distance down from each shoulder.)

4 Transfer the Love pattern from page 80 onto the front of your shirt. Line up the centerline of the pattern with the centerline on your shirt.

5 Place the #20 plunger into the Be-Dazzler machine and turn the setter plate to #20. Insert a #20 gold flathead stud at each mark of the design.

Rhinestone T-shirt

Project 2

Seven rhinestones in four rows... here's a simple yet elegant project. Make this shirt to wear day or night; either way, you'll look fabulous!

▲▼◂▲▼◂▲▼◂▲▼◂▲▼◂▲▼◂▲▼◂▲▼◂▲▼◂▲▼◂▲▼◂▲▼◂▲▼◂▲▼◂▲▼◂▲▼◂▲▼◂

Designed by Elaine Schmidt

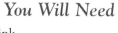

You Will Need

- ◎ T-shirt, pink
- ◎ 7 #60 red rhinestones with settings
- ◎ 7 #60 purple rhinestones with settings
- ◎ 7 #60 blue rhinestones with settings
- ◎ 7 #60 green rhinestones with settings
- ◎ Vanishing fabric marker
- ◎ Ruler

Note: Hat instructions can be found page 42.

This design looks great on young girls, too! Instead of rows of seven rhinestones, use only five.

1 Turn the T-shirt inside out. Find the center of the shirt by folding it in half. Mark the center-line with the vanishing fabric marker, as shown on page 13.

2 Open the shirt again and lay it flat on your work surface.

3 Decide how far down from the neckline you would like the design to go. Set the edge of the ruler where you want to mark the top row of rhinestones. Check that the ruler is straight on the shirt. Line up the 6" mark of the ruler with the centerline marked in Step 1 on the shirt.

4 Draw a small dot on the shirt just above the ruler at the 3", 4", 5", 6", 7", 8" and 9" marks. You should now have a straight row of seven equally spaced dots across the shirt.

5 Move the ruler down about 3/4" and make another row of seven dots, just under the first row.

6 Move the ruler down about 1-1/4" and make another row of seven dots.

7 Move the ruler down about 3/4" and make the last row of seven dots. At this point, check your design and make any corrections if needed.

8 Place the #60 plunger into the Be-Dazzler machine and turn the setter plate to #20. Insert a row of #60 red rhinestones along the top row of your design. Complete the design with a row of purple rhinestones, a row of blue rhinestones, and a row of green rhinestones.

9 Turn the shirt back to the right side and check that all of the tiffany settings are secure around each rhinestone.

Pretty in Purple T-shirt

Swirls of silver studs turn this simple T-shirt into a stunning design.

Designed by Nancy Keller

You Will Need

- T-shirt, purple
- Studded Neckline patterns
- 85 #20 silver pearl studs
- 16 #40 silver pearl studs
- Heart & Flower Stud Pack (6 small hearts, 3 flower studs, 1 large heart stud)
- Custom Hand Tool
- Vanishing fabric marker
- Ruler

Note: See photo at left for stud placement.

1 Find the center of the T-shirt by folding it in half. Mark the centerline with the vanishing fabric marker, as shown on page 13.

2 Open the shirt again and lay it flat on your work surface.

3 Decide how far down from the neckline you would like the design to go. With the ruler and vanishing fabric marker, draw a line, indicating the top of your design. (Check that your line is straight by measuring the same distance down from each shoulder.)

4 Transfer the Studded Neckline patterns on pages 80 and 81 onto the shirt.

5 Place the #20 plunger into the Be-Dazzler machine and turn the setter plate to #20. Insert the #20 studs into the shirt, along the neckline and on the marked design.

6 Place the #40 plunger into the Be-Dazzler machine and turn the setter plate to #40. Insert the #40 studs into the shirt.

7 Place the #60 plunger into the Be-Dazzler machine and turn the setter plate to #20. Insert the flower studs into the shirt.

8 Using the Custom Hand Tool, insert the small and large hearts into the shirt.

Western Denim Shirt

Project 4

We have roped up a great design for you to Be-Dazzle that plain denim shirt hanging in your closet. It's so darn easy even a "greenhorn" stud-setter can do it!

Designed by Marci Metzler

You Will Need

- Denim shirt
- Small Star, Small Boot, Large Boot, and Howdy patterns
- Western Stud Pack (6 silver square studs with stars and 6 large round silver studs with stars)
- 74 silver small stars
- 315 #20 silver flathead studs
- 2 #20 silver textured pearl studs
- 6 silver large stars
- Custom Hand Tool

1 With the Custom Hand Tool, set a row of #40 stars along the border of the shirt collar.

2 With the Custom Hand Tool, set a large round stud with a star between each of the shirt's buttonholes.

3 Place the #20 plunger into the Be-Dazzler machine and turn the setter plate to #20. Set a row of #20 flathead studs along both shoulder seams.

4 Transfer the Small Star pattern on page 81 onto the front of the shirt, below the right shoulder.

5 Set a #20 flathead stud at each circle of the pattern. With the Custom Hand Tool, set a small star at each asterisk around the pattern and a large star at the center asterisk.

6 Transfer the Small Boot pattern on page 81 onto the front of the shirt, below the left shoulder. Set a #20 flathead stud at each open circle on the pattern. Set a #20 textured pearl stud at the black circles on the pattern. Set a small star at each asterisk on the pattern with the Custom Hand Tool.

7 On each of the front pockets, set a row of #20 flathead studs along the bottom edge. On the flap of each pocket, set a border of small stars with the Custom Hand Tool, as well as three square studs with a star.

8 On the back of the shirt, set a row of large stars along the horizontal seam with the Custom Hand Tool.

9 Transfer the Howdy pattern on page 82 onto the back of the shirt, below the row of stars. Place the design at an angle as shown. Set a #20 flathead stud at each circle on the pattern. Set a small star at each asterisk with the Custom Hand Tool.

10 Transfer the Large Boot pattern on page 83 onto the back of the shirt, below "Howdy." Set a #20 flathead stud at each circle on the pattern. Set a small star at each asterisk with the Custom Hand Tool.

Come Play Shirt and Capris

Instant fun, instant allure, instant outfit… that's what you'll have when you make this shirt and pants set with your Be-Dazzler!

Designed by Sandy Dye

You Will Need

- Shirt, green
- Capri pants, black
- Retro Stud Pack (7 happy face studs)
- 110 silver triangle studs
- 54 #20 silver flathead studs
- 115 #20 silver pearl studs
- Custom Hand Tool
- Vanishing fabric marker
- Ruler

This style also looks wonderful on young girls. Instead of creating four flowers on the shirt front, make only three.

1 Use the ruler and measure up from the bottom of the shirt, 6" for the center of the first flower. Make a small mark on the shirt with the vanishing fabric marker at that point. Move over about 2" to 3" and measure up from the bottom of the shirt, 9" for the center of the next flower. Move over 2" and measure up from the bottom of the shirt, 8" for the center of the third flower. Move over 2" to 3" and measure up 6" for the center of the last flower.

2 Place the #60 plunger into the Be-Dazzler machine and turn the setter plate to #20. Insert a happy face stud at each mark on the shirt in Step 1.

3 With the Custom Hand Tool, set seven triangle studs around each happy face center. Notice how one corner of each triangle stud points toward the center of the flower. On the last flower, only set five triangle studs.

4 Place the #20 plunger into the Be-Dazzler machine and turn the setter plate to #20. Create a stem for each flower with #20 pearl studs. Let the stems of the flower bend and wiggle a little bit—don't try to make them straight! With the vanishing fabric marker, mark where you want the leaves to go on the side of the stems. Use #20 flat-head studs to create the leaves.

5 Create a border design on the cuff of each sleeve with triangle studs, using the Custom Hand Tool. Make a pattern with the studs, following the edge of the cuff: one triangle pointing up, the next pointing down. Start the border at the seam at the back of the sleeve so that when you set the last stud, any break in your pattern will be less noticeable.

6 Decorate one leg of the capri pants with three flowers. Measure 6" up from the bottom of one pant leg and mark the center of the first flower. Make another flower center 8" up from the bottom and the last flower 5". Depending upon the width of the pant leg, space out the flowers so that there is enough room to insert the petals. Follow Steps 3 and 4 to complete the flower design. Stop each stem at least 2" before the bottom of the leg to leave room for the border design.

7 Create a border on both pant legs. Follow Step 5 to create this design.

Star-studded Shirt and Bell Bottoms

Star light, star bright: that's the astronomical statement you'll be making when you create this star-studded shirt and "streaming" jeans. Make them today and shine tonight!

Designed by NSI Innovations

You Will Need for Shirt

- Shirt, yellow
- Zigzag Star pattern
- 200 #20 silver round diamond cut studs
- 75 #20 gold pearl studs
- 12 #20 silver pearl studs
- 6 gold small stars
- Ruler
- Vanishing fabric marker
- Custom Hand Tool

1 Find the center of the shirt by folding it in half. Mark the centerline with the vanishing fabric marker, as shown on page 13.

2 Open the shirt again and lay it flat on your work surface.

3 Transfer the Zigzag Star pattern on page 83 onto the front of the shirt. Line up the centerline of the transfer with the centerline on the shirt.

4 Place the #20 plunger into the Be-Dazzler machine and turn the setter plate to #20.

5 At each mark outlining the star, insert a #20 silver round diamond cut stud. Fill in the star with additional #20 silver round diamond cut studs. Set the studs close to each other, creating a tightly filled studded star on the shirt.

6 Set a #20 gold pearl stud on each mark along the five wavy lines around the star.

7 Set #20 gold pearl studs along the neckline of the shirt. Set the studs about 3/4" apart.

8 Alternate #20 gold and #20 silver pearl studs along the cuff of each arm. Set these studs about 3/4" apart.

9 With the Custom Hand Tool, set six gold stars around the star design on the front of the shirt.

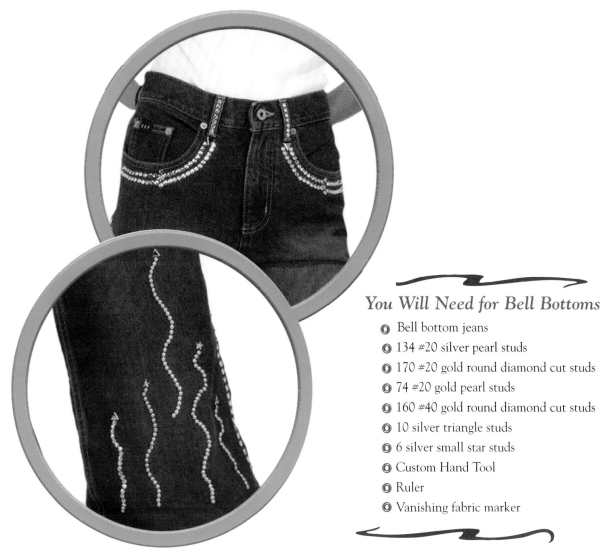

1 Set a triangle stud just under the belt loop near the front pocket using the Custom Hand Tool.

2 Place the #20 plunger into the Be-Dazzler machine and turn the setter plate to #20. Set a row of #20 silver diamond cut studs along the opening of the front pocket. When you get to the middle of the row, set the stud a little higher than the rest to allow room for the star.

3 With the Custom Hand Tool, insert a small star under the middle stud and another triangle stud at the other end of the pocket opening.

4 Set a row of #20 gold diamond cut studs below the silver studs, dropping the middle stud below the star.

5 With the Custom Hand Tool, set a row of #20 gold diamond cut studs along each belt loop.

6 Set a long row of #40 gold diamond cut studs down the outside seam of each pant leg. You may need to use the Custom Hand Tool for this, especially if the seam is very thick.

7 Lay one of the legs of the jeans on a flat work surface. Using the ruler and vanishing fabric marker, mark a design on the leg. Create five wavy lines, starting four of the lines 2" up from the hem of the leg. Start the middle line 7" up from the bottom. Make one line 5" long, the second line 7", the middle line 7", the fourth line 9", and the fifth line 5". Do not try to make the lines straight! Wiggle them a little as shown.

8 Set a row of #20 gold diamond cut studs along the first and fifth lines. Set the studs close together along your wavy line. Set a row of #20 silver pearl studs along the second and fourth lines. Set a row of #20 gold pearl studs along the middle line.

9 With the Custom Hand Tool, add a triangle stud above the first, third, and fifth lines. Add a small star above the second and fourth lines.

10 Repeat Steps 8 to 10 for the other leg.

Beaded, Fringed Capri Jeans and T-shirt

Here is a pretty outfit just brimming with life and light! And it's so easy, too: turn any T-shirt and any pair of pants into a matching set with your Be-Dazzler and Cool Coordinates!

▲▼◄▲▼◄▲▼◄▲▼◄▲▼◄▲▼◄▲▼◄▲▼◄▲▼◄▲▼◄▲▼◄▲▼◄▲▼◄▲▼◄▲▼◄

Designed by Elaine Schmidt

You Will Need

- ◎ Capri jeans, white
- ◎ T-shirt, white
- ◎ Be-Dazzler Cool Coordinates, Rainbow Extras Trim Pack
- ◎ 17 #40 assorted colored rhinestones with settings (**Note:** The trim pack provides 10 rhinestones; 7 additional #40 rhinestones will be needed.)
- ◎ Ruler
- ◎ Vanishing fabric marker
- ◎ Fabric glue
- ◎ Straight pin
- ◎ Scissors

Note: Headband instructions can be found page 43. Belt instructions can be found on page 44.

1 To embellish the bottom of the capri pants, glue beaded fringe trim all around the bottom edge of each leg.

2 Attach ribbon trim over the fabric edge of the fringe trim on each leg. Use fabric glue to attach the ribbon. **Note:** The ribbon ends should overlap at the back of the leg where it will be less noticeable. Turn the overlapping end under as you glue it down to prevent it from fraying.

3 Place the #20 plunger into the Be-Dazzler machine and turn the setter plate to #20. Set a row of #20 pearl studs above the ribbon trim. Leave about 1" between each stud.

4 Using fabric glue, attach three butterfly appliqués on the front of each leg. Leave space for a rhinestone to be set between each appliqué.

5 Insert a straight pin through the leg where you want one of the rhinestones to go. Look inside the leg where the pin is coming through and mark that point with the vanishing fabric marker. Do this for each rhinestone placement.

6 Place the #40 plunger into the Be-Dazzler machine and turn the setter plate to #40. Turn the legs inside out and set a #40 rhinestone at each mark.

7 Set a border of #40 rhinestones along the opening of both front pockets.

8 To decorate the neckline of the T-shirt, alternate #40 rhinestones and #20 pearl studs below the ribbed neckline. Follow the procedure in Step 5 to mark rhinestone placement, leaving 2" between each for the studs. Turn the shirt inside out and set the rhinestones first. Turn the shirt to the right side and insert the studs between the rhinestones.

Swirl and Whirl Shirt and Skirt

11-12

Just think! With a shirt and skirt set like this, you could be out on the floor tonight dancing up a storm in the creation you made this morning!

Designed by Sandy Dye

You Will Need

- Shirt, black
- Skirt, black
- Swirl 1 and Swirl 2 patterns
- 131 #40 clear rhinestones with settings
- 140 #20 clear rhinestones with settings
- Ruler
- Vanishing fabric marker

1 To embellish the shirt, turn it inside out and lay it on a flat work surface.

2 First transfer the Swirl 2 pattern on page 84 onto the inside of the shirt. Start the top of the design at the right shoulder.

3 Now transfer the Swirl 1 pattern on page 84 onto the shirt. Match up the part of the design below the line to the design already on the shirt.

4 Place the #40 plunger into the Be-Dazzler machine and turn the setter plate to #40. At each mark on the inside of the shirt, set a #40 clear rhinestone.

5 Place the #20 plunger into the Be-Dazzler machine and turn the setter plate to #20. Set a border of #20 clear rhinestones along the bottom edge of each sleeve.

6 To embellish the skirt, turn it inside out and lay it on a flat work surface.

7 Transfer the entire Swirl 1 pattern on page 84 onto the inside of the skirt, on the right-hand side.

8 Place the #40 plunger into the Be-Dazzler machine and turn the setter plate to #40. Set a #40 clear rhinestone at each mark of the swirl.

9 Place the #20 plunger into the Be-Dazzler machine and turn the setter plate to #20. Set a border of #20 clear rhinestones along the bottom of the skirt.

Studded Jeans

Project 13

Designed by NSI Innovations

What a great look—and what a cool way to get it! You're just seven easy steps away from a pair of jeans that are almost as unique as you.

You Will Need

- Jeans
- Be-Dazzler Cool Coordinates, Denim Accents Trim Pack (6 silver square flower studs)
- 46 #20 silver round diamond cut studs (**Note:** The Trim Pack includes 30 #20 studs.)
- Custom Hand Tool
- Fabric glue or hot iron
- Scissors

Note: Shoe instructions can be found on page 50.

1 Place the #20 plunger into the Be-Dazzler machine and turn the setter plate to #20. Following the opening of each front pocket, insert a row of #20 round diamond cut studs. **Note:** Pull the inside pocket material out of the way when you insert the studs!

2 Attach a butterfly appliqué under each pocket opening. Adhered the appliqués to the jeans with a hot iron or fabric glue, following the directions that come with the Trim Pack.

3 On the bottom of each pant leg, insert a row of #20 round diamond cut studs. Make the row of studs about 2" up from the bottom edge of the leg. Decorate only the front of each pant leg.

4 With the Custom Hand Tool, insert a row of three square flower studs above the round diamond cut studs.

5 Attach two butterfly appliqués to each leg.

6 Attach fringe trim all around the bottom edge of each pant leg. Use fabric glue to attach the trim.

7 Using fabric glue, attach ribbon trim over the fabric edge of the fringe trim to complete the decoration. **Note:** The ribbon ends should overlap at the back of the leg where it will be less noticeable. Turn the overlapping end under as you glue it down to prevent the end from fraying.

Pink Fringed Jeans

Project 14

Designed by NSI Innovations

Pink suede-like fringe, studs, and rhinestones add just the right amount of sparkle to deep, dark denim.

You Will Need

- Jeans
- Be-Dazzler Cool Coordinates, Burgundy Blast Trim Pack (16 #20 diamond cut studs and 8 #40 pink rhinestones with settings)
- Fabric glue or hot iron
- Vanishing fabric marker
- Straight pin
- Scissors

1 Insert a straight pin through the leg where you want the first rhinestone to go, about 2" up from the bottom edge of the leg. Look inside the leg where the pin is coming through and mark that point with the vanishing fabric marker. Do this for each rhinestone placement.

2 Place the #40 plunger into the Be-Dazzler machine and turn the setter plate to #40. Insert rhinestones into the jeans in the marks made in Step 1.

3 Now, place the #20 plunger into the Be-Dazzler machine and turn the setter plate to #20. Insert #20 studs into the jeans, about 3" up from the bottom edge of the leg and between the rhinestones set in Step 2.

4 Attach fringe trim all around the bottom edge of each pant leg. Use fabric glue to attach the trim.

5 Using fabric glue, attach ribbon trim over the fabric edge of the fringe trim to complete the decoration. **Note:** The ribbon ends should overlap at the back of the leg where it will be less noticeable. Turn the overlapping end under as you glue it down to prevent the end from fraying.

6 Using fabric glue or a hot iron and following the directions that come with the Trim Pack, adhere three ladybug appliqués around each front pocket, leaving space for one stud between them.

7 With the Be-Dazzler machine still set at #20, place one #20 diamond cut stud between each ladybug.

Flower Power Jeans

Project 15

You might expect to pay at least a hundred dollars for custom jeans like these, but with some time and planning, this pair can be made at a fraction of the cost!

Designed by Elaine Schmidt

You Will Need

- Jeans
- 62 silver triangle studs
- 62 #60 silver flat diamond studs
- Custom Hand Tool
- 54 #20 silver pearl studs
- 227 #40 silver pearl studs
- 90 #60 silver pearl studs

Note: These jeans are created freeform, so detailed directions are not given. In general, the leaves are outlined with #40 studs, and a line of #20 studs serves as the leaf "vein." The bonus Large Leaf pattern on page 89 gives you the general shape. The flowers are formed with a round stud center and then either triangle or diamond studs surround the center as petals.

1 Place the #40 plunger into the Be-Dazzler machine and turn the setter plate to #40. Insert a row of #40 pearl studs around each front pocket.

2 Place the #60 plunger into the Be-Dazzler machine and turn the setter plate to #20. Insert #60 pearl studs down the side seams of the jeans.

3 With the Be-Dazzler machine still set for #60 studs, use #60 pearl studs at the beginning of the flower stems and at the center of the larger flowers.

4 Place the #40 plunger into the Be-Dazzler machine and turn the setter plate to #40. Insert the #40 pearl studs for the leaves and for the middle sections of the stems. Also use #40 studs for

the centers of the smaller flowers.

5 Place the #20 plunger into the Be-Dazzler machine and turn the setter plate to #20. Insert the #20 pearl studs for the center of the leaves and upper sections of the stems (Note how the stems use #60 at the bottom and then gradually use #40 and then #20).

6 Using the Custom Hand Tool, insert six triangle studs around each #60 pearl stud to create the flower petals. Have one point of each triangle point toward the pearl stud.

7 Using the Custom Hand Tool, insert six diamond studs around each #40 pearl stud for the smaller flowers.

Stars and Stripes Jean Jacket

Project 16

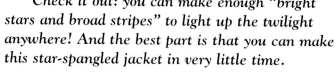

Check it out: you can make enough "bright stars and broad stripes" to light up the twilight anywhere! And the best part is that you can make this star-spangled jacket in very little time.

Designed by Elaine Schmidt

You Will Need

- Jean jacket
- 56 #60 red rhinestones with settings
- 23 #60 blue rhinestones with settings
- 42 #40 silver pearl studs
- 34 #60 silver square domed studs
- 52 silver small stars
- 46 #40 red rhinestones with settings
- Custom Hand Tool
- Ruler
- Vanishing fabric marker

1 With the Custom Hand Tool, insert triangle studs above and below each buttonhole. Make the triangles point away from the buttonholes.

2 Insert a triangle stud on each collar tip. Make the triangles point toward the tip.

3 Insert a row of small stars across the horizontal seam above the pocket on both sides of the jacket front using the Custom Hand Tool.

4 Place the #40 plunger into the Be-Dazzler machine and turn the setter plate to #40. Insert a row of #40 rhinestones above the row of stars. Look at the inside of the jacket. The row of stars will be evident by the prongs secured into the back of the fabric. With the inside of the jacket facing up, place the row of rhinestones above the row of prongs.

6 Insert small stars along the edge of the collar, leaving about 1-1/4" space between each star. With the inside of the jacket facing up, set a #40 rhinestone between each star.

7 Turn the jacket to the back. With the Custom Hand Tool, set a row of square domed studs all around the back yoke and shoulder seam lines.

8 Turn the jacket inside out. With a ruler and the vanishing fabric marker, mark a grid for the flag design under the back yoke. Draw nine horizontal lines and thirteen vertical lines. Each line should be 3/4" apart. Begin the horizontal lines about 1-1/4" down from the horizontal seam of the back yoke. Begin the vertical lines by measuring the entire width of the center back panel and determining where the center is. Draw the center vertical line, and then draw six vertical lines on each side of the centerline.

9 Place the #60 plunger into the Be-Dazzler machine and turn the setter plate to #20. Using the photo above as a guide and following the intersections marked in Step 8, insert #60 blue and #60 red rhinestones into the jacket.

10 Turn to the right side of the jacket again. Complete the flag design by inserting #40 pearl studs and small stars (with the Custom Hand Tool) as shown.

11 Around each cuff, alternate square-domed studs with #60 red rhinestones.

12 Around the bottom of the entire jacket, alternate a small star (with the Custom Hand Tool), a #40 red rhinestone, and a #60 blue rhinestone, changing the Be-Dazzler settings for each different size.

Trimmed and Studded Jean Jacket

Studs, appliqués, fringe, and retro trim: goodies galore! This fun jacket has a '60s feel you are going to love!

Designed by Elaine Schmidt

You Will Need

- Jean jacket
- Be-Dazzler Cool Coordinates, Denim Accents Trim Pack
- Fabric glue
- Retro Stud Pack
- 72 #60 mirror studs
- 72 #60 silver square domed studs
- Custom Hand Tool
- Scissors

1 With fabric glue, attach fringe trim to the underside of the collar. To do this, glue the fabric edge of the trim to the edge of the collar. Only the fringe should appear when the collar is turned down.

2 Cut a piece of fringe trim to fit the shoulder seam on each side of the jacket and attach with fabric glue.

3 Attach a piece of ribbon trim to the horizontal seam just under the yoke on both sides of the jacket front. Cut the ribbon trim about 1" longer than needed. Fold back the ends of the ribbon trim 1/2" on each side to create a finished edge. Glue the folded ends to the back of the ribbon. Glue the ribbon to the jacket.

4 With the Custom Hand Tool, insert a row of square domed studs above the ribbon trim.

5 Set the Be-Dazzler machine with the #60 plunger and a #20 setting. Insert a row of mirror studs above the square domed studs. To insert mirror studs, place the ring of the stud inside the plunger. Lower the arm of the machine over the fabric and carefully position the mirror over the plastic disk on the fabric just before pressing down on the plunger.

6 Keeping the #20 setting on the machine, insert a happy face stud between each buttonhole of the jacket.

7 Attach a butterfly appliqué to each side of the jacket front with fabric glue. Insert a butterfly stud on one side of the jacket, using the Custom Hand Tool. Insert a peace sign stud to each collar tip with the Custom Hand Tool.

8 Turn the jacket to the back. Attach a piece of ribbon across the horizontal seam below the yoke of the jacket. Cut the ribbon 1" longer than needed to fold back the ends as described in Step 3.

9 Insert a row of square domed studs all around the back yoke with the Custom Hand Tool. Insert a row of mirrors inside the border of square studs, as described in Step 5.

10 Insert a row of mirrors down the back seam of each arm.

11 To complete the jacket, add square domed studs around each cuff and along the bottom of the jacket with the Custom Hand Tool.

Straw Hat With Ribbon Trim

Hats are real attention-grabbers! Adorn a wide-brimmed straw hat with silver star and pearl studs and you're sure to get many admiring glances.

Designed by Nancy Keller

You Will Need

- Wide brim straw hat
- 1-1/2" wide ribbon, black
- 90 #20 silver textured pearl studs
- 20 silver small star studs
- Custom Hand Tool
- Fabric glue
- Ruler
- Vanishing fabric marker
- Scissors

1 Measure and cut a piece of ribbon to fit around the hat with some overlap.

2 Using the ruler and vanishing fabric marker, make a row of dots along the top edge of the ribbon. Make the dots about 3/4" apart. Make a similar row of dots along the bottom edge of the ribbon.

3 Make a middle row of dots on the ribbon, but these dots should line up under the spaces of the row above.

4 Place the #20 plunger into the Be-Dazzler machine and turn the setter plate to #20. Place a #20 textured pearl stud at every dot along the top and bottom row of the ribbon. For the middle row, insert a #20 textured pearl at every other dot (skipping over one dot between each stud).

5 Set small star studs on the remaining marks of the middle row using the Custom Hand Tool.

6 Wrap the studded ribbon around the hat, using fabric glue to seal the ribbon where it overlaps.

7 For the bow, cut one 13" piece of ribbon, one 10" piece of ribbon, and one 3-1/2" piece of ribbon.

8 Loop the 13" ribbon around so that the ends overlap. Glue the overlapping ends together. Loop the 10" ribbon the same way and glue the overlapping ends together. For the center of the 3-1/2" ribbon, mark and set four textured pearl studs with a star in the center.

9 Position the 10" looped ribbon in front of the 13" looped ribbon. Wrap the 3-1/2" piece of ribbon around both to create the bow. Glue the ends of this piece together at the back of the bow.

10 Glue the bow onto the hat, covering the spot where the ribbon overlaps.

Soft Denim Hat

Project 19

Designed by Elaine Schmidt

Looking for an easy way to create a new look for an old hat? Whether you have a green thumb or not, you'll love making the silver and rhinestone flowers bloom!

You Will Need

- Soft denim hat
- Simple Flower pattern
- 4 large silver heart studs
- 81 #20 silver flathead studs
- 27 #40 assorted colored rhinestones with settings
- 6 small silver flowers
- Custom Hand Tool
- Ruler
- Vanishing fabric marker

Note: T-Shirt instructions can be found page 22.

1 Along the inside of the hat's rim, use the vanishing fabric marker and indicate three dots in a row (about 1" apart), then leave a space of about 2", and repeat the three dots again. Continue to repeat this pattern of three dots, then a space around the entire rim of the hat.

2 Place the #40 plunger into the Be-Dazzler machine and turn the setter plate to #40. At each dot on the inside of the rim of the hat, insert a #40 rhinestone with a tiffany setting.

3 In the spaces left between the groups of rhinestones, alternate heart studs and small flower studs. The heart studs should be inserted with the Custom Hand Tool. The small flower studs can be inserted with the Be-Dazzler machine with the #60 plunger and #20 setting.

4 Transfer the Simple Flower pattern on page 85 to the hat three times to make three studded flowers. Use #20 flathead studs to create the flowers, as marked on the pattern (the open circles).

5 When the #20 flathead studs are all inserted, turn the hat inside out and locate the center of each flower design. It should not be too hard to find the center—the prongs of the flathead studs create the same design inside the hat.

6 Place the #40 plunger into the Be-Dazzler machine and turn the setter plate to #40. Keeping the hat inside out, insert a #40 rhinestone at the center of each flower.

Studded Headband

Embellishing a plain headband is quick and easy—just one step and you are done!

▲▼◄▲▼◄▲▼◄▲▼◄▲▼◄▲▼◄▲▼◄▲▼◄▲▼◄▲▼◄▲▼◄▲▼◄▲▼◄▲▼◄▲▼

Designed by Elaine Schmidt

Project 20

Note: T-Shirt instructions can be found page 31.

You Will Need

- Headband, pink
- 15 #60 silver flathead studs

1 Place the #60 plunger into the Be-Dazzler machine and turn the setter plate to #20. Insert one line of studs all of the way around the headband, spacing the studs about 1-1/4" apart.

Punky Belt, Choker, and Cuffs

Projects
21·22·23

A tribute to the 1980s, this accessory set looks perfect with a simple outfit. Each piece is made from webbing that can be purchased at any fabric store.

▼◀▲◀▼◀▲◀▼◀▲◀▼◀▲◀▼◀▲◀▼◀▲◀▼◀▲◀▼

Designed by Elaine Schmidt

You Will Need for Belt

◉ 1-1/4" wide webbing, black, in length to fit around waist plus 8"
◉ D-ring buckle
◉ 56 #40 silver flathead studs
◉ Fabric glue or needle and thread

Note: Jeans and T-shirt instructions can be found page 31.

You Will Need for Choker

◉ 1" wide webbing, black, in length to fit around neck, plus a little overlap
◉ 12 silver square domed studs
◉ Custom Hand Tool
◉ Velcro

1 Loop one end of the webbing through the D-ring and sew or glue to hold. Fold a bit of the other end of the webbing to the back and sew or glue to hold (to prevent fraying).

2 Try on the belt to see what area will go through the D-ring; do not insert studs here. Note that when the belt is worn, the opposite side of the webbing shows at the short end, so set the studs in this section on the back side.

3 Place the #40 plunger into the Be-Dazzler machine and turn the setter plate to #40. Insert two studs, one on top of the other, in rows about 1" apart.

1 Adhere Velcro to the ends of the webbing.

2 Using the Custom Hand Tool, insert one line of studs all of the way around the entire choker, each about 1-1/4" apart.

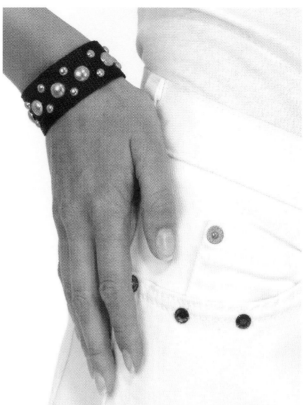

You Will Need for Cuff 1

- 2" wide webbing, black, in length to fit around wrist plus a little overlap
- 8 #60 pearl studs
- 18 silver triangle studs
- Custom Hand Tool
- Velcro

You Will Need for Cuff 2

- 1" wide webbing, navy blue, in length to fit around wrist plus a little overlap
- 8 #40 silver textured pearl studs
- 14 #20 textured pearl studs
- Velcro

1 Adhere Velcro to the ends of the webbing.

2 Place the #60 plunger into the Be-Dazzler machine and turn the setter plate to #20. Insert the pearl studs into the center of the cuff, all of the way around. Space the studs about 1" apart.

3 Using the Custom Hand Tool, insert two triangle studs in the spaces between the studs, one on top of the other, as shown.

1 Adhere Velcro to the ends of the webbing.

2 Place the #40 plunger into the Be-Dazzler machine and turn the setter plate to #40. Insert the #40 pearl studs into the center of the cuff, all of the way around. Space the studs about 1" apart.

3 Place the #20 plunger into the Be-Dazzler machine and turn the setter plate to #20. Insert two #20 pearl studs in the spaces between the studs, one on top of the other, as shown.

8 Snowflakes and Stars Shawl

Designed by Nancy Keller

Project 24

Looking for the perfect gift to give to a friend—or to yourself? Here's a gem of a shawl for any special occasion, or just to cuddle up in on a cool night.

You Will Need

- Large rectangular shawl, purple
- 42 #40 clear rhinestones with settings
- 110 silver triangle studs
- 50 silver flat diamond studs
- 54 silver small star studs
- Custom Hand Tool
- Vanishing fabric marker
- Ruler

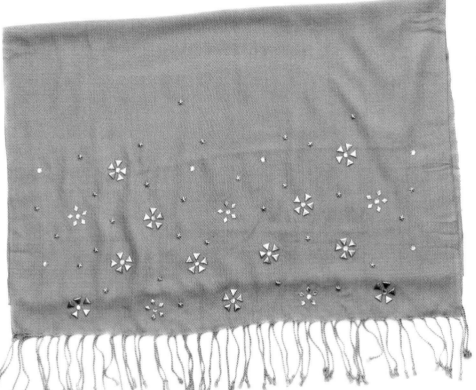

1 Lay one end of the shawl on a table with the wrong side facing up.

2 Using the ruler and vanishing fabric marker, mark a row of dots along the bottom edge of the shawl. Start the row of dots 2" up from the edge of the shawl and leave about 5" of space between each dot.

3 Make a second row of dots, this time 5" up from the edge of the shawl. Begin the first dot over the first space of the row below.

4 Make a third row of dots 6" up from the first row. Complete the design with two dots above the third row.

5 Repeat Steps 1 to 4, making the same pattern of dots at the other end of the shawl.

6 Place the #40 plunger into the Be-Dazzler machine and turn the setter plate to #40. At each dot on the back of the shawl, insert a #40 clear rhinestone with a tiffany setting.

7 With the Custom Hand Tool, insert five triangle shaped studs around the first rhinestone of the bottom row. Insert five flat diamond studs around the next rhinestone. Alternate these two snowflake designs around each of the rhinestones on the shawl.

8 Complete the design by adding star studs (with the Custom Hand Tool) and clear rhinestones at random around the snowflakes.

9 Repeat Steps 6 to 8 for the other end of the shawl.

Red Scarf and Bag

Projects 25-26

Designed by Sandy Dye

The combination of trims from the Rainbow Extras Cool Coordinates and lots of silver studs is perfect for this cute summery set.

You Will Need for Scarf and Bag

- Scarf and bag, red
- Medallion pattern
- Be-Dazzler Cool Coordinates, Rainbow Extras Trim Pack
- 36 #40 gold flathead studs
- 12 #40 gold diamond cut studs
- 14 silver triangle studs
- 26 silver flat diamond studs
- 2 #60 flower studs
- Fabric glue
- Scissors
- Custom Hand Tool

Scarf

1 Transfer the Medallion pattern on page 85 onto the scarf, near the tip of the triangle.

2 Using the Custom Hand Tool, place one flower stud into the center of the motif.

3 Using the Custom Hand Tool, place six diamond studs into the motif, as shown.

4 Using the Custom Hand Tool, insert six triangle studs into the motif, as shown.

5 Place the #40 plunger into the Be-Dazzler machine and turn the setter plate to #40. Insert eighteen gold flathead studs into the motif, as shown.

6 Using the Custom Hand Tool, place fourteen diamond studs along the long end of the scarf.

7 Using fabric glue, adhere the trim around two sides of the scarf, as shown.

Bag

1 Transfer the Medallion pattern on page 85 onto the bag, near the top.

2 Follow Steps 2 to 5 for the Scarf to create the Medallion motif.

3 About 1" below the design, adhere a line of ribbon with fabric glue.

4 About 1-1/2" below the ribbon, adhere a line of fringe trim.

5 Using the Custom Hand Tool, insert the remaining two triangle studs into the bag, between the ribbon and fringe trim.

utterfly Tote Bag

Project 27

You've always got stuff to carry, so why not do it in style? Here's the ultimate tote bag design you can make and take in the wink of an eye.

Designed by Elaine Schmidt

You Will Need

- Tote bag, dark blue
- Butterfly pattern
- 144 #20 gold flathead studs
- 9 #40 assorted colored rhinestones with settings
- 5 #20 assorted colored rhinestones with settings
- 9 #40 gold flathead studs
- Ruler
- Vanishing fabric marker
- Straight pin

1 Lay the tote bag on a flat work surface. To find the center of the bag, either fold the bag in half or use a ruler. Mark the centerline with the vanishing fabric marker.

2 Transfer the Butterfly pattern on page 85 onto the front of the tote bag, lining up the center of the pattern with the line marked in Step 1.

3 Place the #20 plunger into the Be-Dazzler machine and turn the setter plate to #20. At each open circle on the pattern, set a #20 gold flathead stud.

4 At each asterisk on the pattern, insert a straight pin through the front of the bag. Look inside the bag where the pin is coming through and mark that point with the vanishing fabric marker. Do this for each rhinestone placement.

5 Turn the bag inside out and set a #40 or #20 rhinestone at each mark, changing the Be-Dazzler machine setting for each different size.

6 Turn the tote bag to the right side again. Make a row of dots with the fabric marker 1-1/2" down from the top edge of the bag. Space the dots out every 1-1/2" apart.

7 Place the #40 plunger into the Be-Dazzler machine and turn the setter plate to #40. Set a #40 gold flathead stud at each mark along the top of the bag.

Beaded, Fringed Bag

Project 28

Designed by Elaine Schmidt

No, you can't buy this fun bag—but you can create it quickly and easily with the Be-Dazzler and fabric glue!

▲▼◄▲▼◄▲▼"▲▼◄▲▼◄▲▼◄▲▼◄▲▼◄▲▼◄▲▼◄▲▼◄▲▼◄▲▼◄▲▼◄▲▼◄▲▼◄

You Will Need

- Canvas bag with flap, black
- Be-Dazzler Cool Coordinates, Rainbow Extras Trim Pack
- 15 #40 assorted colored rhinestones with settings
- Ruler
- Vanishing fabric marker
- Fabric glue
- Scissors

1 Open the flap of the bag and lay it on a flat work surface with the inside of the flap facing up.

2 With the ruler, measure 3-1/2" down from the edge of the flap. Use a vanishing fabric marker and make a straight row of dots across the inside of the flap. Leave a space of about 3/4" between each dot.

3 Place the #40 plunger into the Be-Dazzler machine and turn the setter plate to #40. Insert a rhinestone with a setting at each mark on the flap.

4 Measure the width of the flap and cut a piece of ribbon trim about 1" longer than the measurement. Fold back the ends of the ribbon trim 1/2" on each side to create a finished edge. Glue the folded ends to the back of the ribbon.

5 Glue the ribbon trim above the row of rhinestones. Turn the flap to the back and insert a rhinestone at each end of the ribbon.

6 Cut a piece of beaded trim to fit across the width of the flap. Glue the trim below the row of rhinestones.

7 Place the #20 plunger into the Be-Dazzler machine and turn the setter plate to #20. Insert a row of #20 pearl studs across the fabric of the beaded trim.

8 Attach two butterfly appliqués above the ribbon trim with fabric glue.

Fun Fringed Shoes

Designed by Elaine Schmidt

These sandals are so snazzy! Check out how well they match with the jeans on page 34.

You Will Need

- Shoes, black
- Be-Dazzler Cool Coordinates, Denim Accents Trim Pack
- Fabric glue
- Scissors

1 Cut a piece of fringe to fit across the top of each shoe. Attach the trim to each shoe with fabric glue.

2 Cut a piece of ribbon trim about 1" longer than the fringe trim. Fold back the ends of the ribbon trim 1/2" on each side to create a finished edge. Glue the folded ends to the back of the ribbon.

3 Glue the ribbon trim over the top of the fringe trim on each shoe.

4 Glue a butterfly appliqué on top of each shoe.

Easy Tie

Project 30

Designed by Elaine Schmidt

Men of all ages will love the simplicity of this tie!

▲▼◄▲▼◄▲▼◄▲▼◄▲▼◄▲▼◄▲▼◄▲▼◄▲▼◄▲▼◄▲▼◄▲▼◄▲▼◄▲▼◄▲▼◄▲▼◄

You Will Need

- Tie, black
- 1 #60 silver flathead stud
- 2 silver flat diamond studs
- Custom Hand Tool
- Ruler

1 Place the #60 plunger into the Be-Dazzler machine and turn the setter plate to #20. Insert the #60 flathead stud into the tie, about 1-1/2" from the tip.

2 Using the Custom Hand Tool, insert one diamond stud above the #60 flathead stud. Insert the remaining diamond stud below the #60 flathead stud.

Simple Studded Jean Jacket

Project 31

By using just two types of studs, this simple design has lots of impact!

You Will Need

- Jean jacket
- 33 #60 silver flathead studs
- 24 silver triangle studs
- Custom Hand Tool

1 Alternating between triangle studs and #60 flathead studs, insert a row of studs across the front chest seamline, leaving about 2" between the studs. Use the Custom Hand Tool to set the triangle studs and the Be-Dazzler machine with the #60 plunger and #20 settler plate to set the #60 flathead studs.

2 Along each lower front pocket (in a row), insert triangle studs on the outside edges with a #60 flathead stud between them.

3 Insert studs along each shoulder seamline, starting with a triangle at the outside and alternating with #60 flathead studs.

4 Turn the jacket over to the back. Again alternating between triangle studs and #60 flathead studs, insert a row of studs across the back yoke seamline, leaving about 2" between the studs.

5 Repeat the alternating pattern down the back seamline of each arm.

Section 2
Projects for Your Home

When people think of the Be-Dazzler, most often they envision cool jeans and shirts, like those in Section 1; however, what about adding studs and rhinestones to home décor items and paper? Here, you will find ways to create cards that are perfect to give on special occasions, a cozy polarfleece blanket, and place settings that will make every mealtime memorable.

Note: When making home décor items, it is important to make sure the stud prongs are flat against the back of the fabric to make sure they won't scratch your furniture. If prongs feel a little sharp, you can either paint the bent prongs with fabric paint or glue, sew, or fuse a little ribbon over them (this works well for placemats). Also, note that the actual amount of studs used for each project may vary depending upon the size of your project (i.e. tablecloth or table runner).

"Denim" Card

Project 32

Designed by Elaine Schmidt

This simple card has a very masculine feel; it's perfect for a birthday or special "thank you."

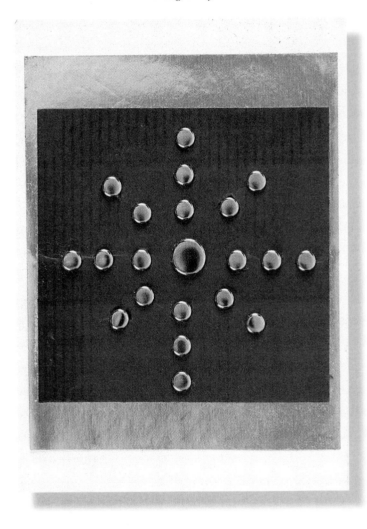

You Will Need

- 3-1/2" x 5" gift card, white
- 3-1/4" x 4" piece of decorative paper, silver
- 3" x 3" piece of decorative paper, blue
- 20 #20 silver flathead studs
- 1 #40 silver flathead stud
- Glue

1 Place the #40 plunger into the Be-Dazzler machine and turn the setter plate to #40. Insert the #40 silver flathead stud into the center of the blue piece of decorative paper.

2 Place the #20 plunger into the Be-Dazzler machine and turn the setter plate to #20. Insert #20 silver flathead studs evenly around the central #40 stud, three at the top, bottom, and sides and two at the "diagonals," as shown.

3 Glue the silver piece of decorative paper onto the center of the gift card.

4 Glue the blue piece of decorative paper onto the center of the silver paper.

Heartfelt Card

Project 33

Wouldn't this simple layered card be perfect for Valentine's Day, or even a wedding?

Designed by Elaine Schmidt

You Will Need

- 5-1/2" x 5-1/2" gift card, purple
- 4-1/2" x 4-1/2" piece of decorative paper, gold
- 4-1/2" x 4-1/2" piece of cardstock, white
- 3-1/2" x 3-1/2" piece of velveteen, red
- 20 #20 silver flathead studs
- Large Heart and Small Heart patterns
- Decorative edge scissors
- 1/8" hole punch
- Scissors
- Pencil
- Glue

1. Trace the Large Heart pattern on page 86 onto the piece of white cardstock. Cut out with decorative edge scissors.

2. Punch holes into the edges of the white heart, as shown.

3. Trace the Small Heart pattern on page 86 onto the piece of red velveteen. Cut out with regular scissors.

4. Place the #20 plunger into the Be-Dazzler machine and turn the setter plate to #20.

Insert #20 silver flathead studs around the outside of the red velveteen heart, as shown.

5. Glue the piece of gold decorative paper onto the center of the purple gift card.

6. Glue the white heart onto the center of the gold paper.

7. Glue the red heart onto the center of the white heart.

Smile Card

Project 34

Designed by Elaine Schmidt

Bright and cheery, this card is sure to bring a smile to the recipient's face!

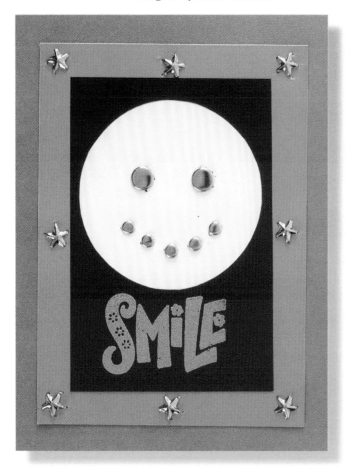

You Will Need

- 5" x 6-3/4" gift card, bright pink
- 4-1/4" x 5-3/4" piece of decorative paper, turquoise
- 3-1/4" x 4-3/4" piece of decorative paper, black
- 3" x 3" piece of decorative paper, bright yellow
- Smile rubber stamp
- Inkpad, turquoise
- 8 silver small stars
- Custom Hand Tool
- 2 #40 silver flathead studs
- 5 #20 silver flathead studs
- Compass
- Scissors
- Glue

1 Using the compass, create a 2-3/4" diameter circle on the bright yellow paper. Cut out.

2 Place the #40 plunger into the Be-Dazzler machine and turn the setter plate to #40. Insert the #40 silver flathead studs onto the yellow circle to create eyes.

3 Place the #20 plunger into the Be-Dazzler machine and turn the setter plate to #20. Insert the #20 silver flathead studs onto the yellow circle to create the mouth.

4 Using the Custom Hand Tool, insert small silver stars onto each corner of the turquoise decorative paper. Now insert studs in the center of the top, bottom, and sides, as shown.

5 Using the rubber stamp and inkpad, stamp "Smile" on the bottom of the black paper, leaving enough space for the yellow circle to be placed above it.

6 Glue the turquoise paper onto the center of the bright pink gift card.

7 Glue the black paper onto the center of the turquoise paper.

8 Glue the yellow circle onto the black paper, above the stamped "Smile."

Vintage Photo Frame

Project 35

This alluring frame captures the simple elegance of days gone by.

Designed by Elaine Schmidt

You Will Need

- 8-1/2" x 11" decorative embossed photo matte, ivory
- 8-1/2" x 11" piece of acid-free paper, ivory
- 4 #40 silver flathead studs
- 36 #20 silver flathead studs
- Photo-safe tape
- Photo-safe glue
- Photo (or photocopy of a photo)

1 Place the #40 plunger into the Be-Dazzler machine and turn the setter plate to #40. Insert #40 silver flathead studs onto the corners of the opening in the ivory photo matte.

2 Place the #20 plunger into the Be-Dazzler machine and turn the setter plate to #20. Insert #20 silver flathead studs evenly spaced around the entire opening in the ivory photo matte.

3 Turn the matte over. Center the photo over the matte's opening and, using photo-safe tape, adhere the photo to the back of the matte.

4 Using photo-safe glue, adhere the piece of acid-free ivory paper onto the back of the matte.

Project 36

Soccer Stars Scrapbook Page

Even though scrapbooking has been around for years, it is as popular as ever. Now you can add panache to your pages with a few randomly placed studs.

▲▼◄▲▼◄▲▼◄▲▼◄▲▼◄▲▼◄▲▼◄▲▼◄▲▼◄▲▼◄▲▼◄▲▼◄▲▼◄▲▼◄▲▼◄▲▼◄▲▼

Designed by Elaine Schmidt

You Will Need

- 12" x 12" piece of acid-free paper, black
- Acid-free paper, white
- 5-1/2" x 4-1/2" and 3-1/2" x 5-3/4" pieces of acid-free paper, black and white striped
- 5 x 4" and 3 x 4-1/2" pieces of acid-free paper, red
- Photo-safe marker, black
- Photo-safe glue
- 13 silver small stars
- Custom Hand Tool
- 69 #20 silver flathead studs
- Compass
- Scissors
- 2 photos
- Ruler

1 Using the compass, cut eleven 1-3/4" diameter circles from the white paper. Cut out.

2 Using the black photo-safe marker, write "SOCCER STARS" on the circles of white paper.

3 Place the #20 plunger into the Be-Dazzler machine and turn the setter plate to #20. Insert #20 silver flathead studs evenly spaced onto each letter, as shown.

4 Cut the photos; one should be 4-1/2" x 3-3/4", and the other should be 2-1/2" x 4".

5 Using photo-safe glue, center the 4-1/2" x 3-3/4" photo onto the 5" x 4" piece of red paper. Glue the red paper onto the 5-1/2" x 4-1/2" piece of black and white striped paper. Repeat the procedure for the remaining photo and pieces of paper.

6 Using photo-safe glue, adhere the matted photos to the black piece of paper at an angle.

7 Using photo-safe glue, adhere the lettered circles onto the black paper, alternating their heights.

8 Using the Custom Hand Tool, insert small silver stars onto the black paper, at random.

Flower Scrapbook Page

This simple page uses pre-cut photo mattes in bright colors, so making it is quick and easy.

Designed by Elaine Schmidt

You Will Need

- 12" x 12" piece of acid-free paper, blue
- 3 flower mattes, in bright colors
- 30 #20 silver flathead studs
- 48 #40 silver flathead studs
- Photo-safe glue
- 3 photos

1 Place the #20 plunger into the Be-Dazzler machine and turn the setter plate to #20. Insert #20 silver flathead studs between the petals of each flower matte.

2 Place the #40 plunger into the Be-Dazzler machine and turn the setter plate to #40. Insert #40 silver flathead studs onto the petal of each flower matte.

3 Turn each flower matte over. Using photo-safe glue, adhere one photo to each flower matte so that the image is centered in the matte's opening.

4 Using photo-safe glue, adhere the three flower mattes to the blue paper, at varying heights.

5 Insert #40 silver flathead studs onto the blue paper, forming straight stems for each of the flowers.

Studded Candles

Project 38

The great thing about these candles is that you don't even need a tool to complete them!

▲▼◄▲▼◄▲▼◄▲▼◄▲▼◄▲▼◄▲▼◄▲▼◄▲▼◄▲▼◄▲▼◄▲▼◄▲▼◄▲▼◄▲▼◄▲▼◄▲▼

Designed by Elaine Schmidt

You Will Need
Option 1

- ◉ 4" tall round candle, green
- ◉ 16 #20 silver flathead studs
- ◉ 16 #60 silver flathead studs
- ◉ 16 silver triangle studs
- ◉ Ruler

1 About 1/2" from the bottom of the candle, begin pressing the #60 studs around the candle, placing each about 1/8" apart.

2 Insert a triangle stud above each #60 stud, with one point pointing upward.

3 Insert one #20 stud directly above each triangle.

You Will Need
Option 2

- ◉ 6" tall round candle, green
- ◉ 32 #20 silver flathead studs
- ◉ 16 #60 silver flathead studs
- ◉ 32 silver triangle studs
- ◉ Ruler

1 About 2-1/2" from the bottom of the candle, begin pressing the #60 studs around the candle, placing each about 1/8" apart.

2 Insert a triangle stud above each #60 stud, with one point pointing upward.

3 Insert a triangle stud below each #60 stud, with one point pointing downward.

4 Insert one #20 stud directly above each "top" triangle.

5 Insert one #20 stud directly below each "bottom" triangle.

Triangle Studded Candle

Project 39

This funky candle is too easy not to try!

▲▼◄▲▼◄▲▼◄▲▼◄▲▼◄▲▼◄▲▼◄▲▼◄▲▼◄▲▼◄▲▼◄▲▼◄▲▼◄▲▼◄▲▼◄▲▼◄

Designed by Elaine Schmidt

You Will Need

- 4" tall round candle, brown
- 80 silver triangle studs
- Ruler

1 About 1-1/2" from the bottom of the candle, begin pressing the triangle studs around the candle. Alternate the way in which the points of each triangle are pointing (upward or downward).

2 About 1-1/2" from the top of the candle, begin pressing the triangle studs around the candle. Alternate the way in which the points of each triangle are pointing (upward or downward).

3 Midway between the top and bottom rows of triangle studs, press the remaining studs about 1" apart, alternating the way in which the point of each triangle is pointing (upward or downward)

Studded Velvet Lampshade

Project 40

Add a touch of light anywhere in your home with this trimmed and studded lampshade.

▽▼◁▲▽◁▲▽◁▲▽◁▲▽◁▲▽◁▲▽◁▲▽◁▲▽◁▲▽◁▲▽◁▲▽◁▲▽◁▲▽◁▲▽◁▲▽

Designed by Elaine Schmidt

You Will Need

- 7 to 15 watt electric candle-stick lamp with shade
- Brushed velvet fabric, green
- Cord trim, gold
- 36 #40 gold diamond cut studs
- 21 #20 gold diamond cut studs
- Fabric glue
- Scissors
- Measuring tape
- Tracing paper
- Tape
- Straight pins
- Pencil

1 Place tracing paper around the lampshade and secure with tape; trace lampshade onto paper to make a pattern. Cut out.

2 Pin the lampshade pattern on a single layer of velvet. Cut out.

3 Place the #40 plunger into the Be-Dazzler machine and turn the setter plate to #40. Set a row of #40 studs approximately 1/2" from the top and bottom of the velvet, spacing them about 1/4" apart.

4 Place the #20 plunger into the Be-Dazzler machine and turn the setter plate to #20. Set a row of #20 studs, spacing them above and between the bottom row of studs, as shown.

5 Glue the studded fabric to the lampshade with fabric glue.

6 Measure lengths of gold cord trim and attach them with glue to the top and bottom of the lampshade.

7 Place tracing paper around the lamp base and secure with tape; trace lamp base onto paper to make a pattern. Cut out.

8 Pin the lamp base pattern on a single layer of velvet. Cut out.

9 Glue the fabric to the lamp base.

Western Lampshade and Tissue Box Cover

Using pre-cut paper pieces make these projects easy to do. While brown gives them a feel of the Old West, choose whatever color works best for your décor.

Designed by Andrea Rothenberg

You Will Need for Lampshade

- Pre-cut paper lampshade, brown
- 21 #60 silver pearl studs
- 9 #60 gold flathead studs
- 36 #60 silver domed square studs
- Custom Hand Tool
- 144 #20 gold diamond cut studs
- Western Star pattern

Note: The lampshade shown has three equal-sized sides. Vary the number of studs accordingly for a different sized or shaped shade. Also, complete one side of the shade first, and then repeat the procedure for each remaining side.

1 Place the #60 plunger into the Be-Dazzler machine and turn the setter plate to #20. Insert #60 silver pearl studs along the top and bottom of the shade; equally space two across the top and four along the bottom.

2 Now insert #60 gold flathead studs onto the shade as shown; these are the centers of each individual design. Place one stud toward the top of the shade and the other two near the bottom, directly across from each other.

3 Follow the Western Star pattern on page 87 and insert the silver domed square studs with the Custom Hand Tool, four around each gold flathead stud. (**Note:** Do not transfer the pattern with an iron onto the paper.)

4 Now place the #20 plunger into the Be-Dazzler machine and turn the setter plate to #20. Insert #20 gold diamond cut studs into the shade, following the pattern.

5 Finally, place the #60 plunger into the Be-Dazzler machine and turn the setter plate to #20. Insert the final #60 silver pearl stud into the shade, between the two bottom designs.

You Will Need for Tissue Box Cover

- Pre-cut paper tissue box cover, brown
- 24 #60 silver pearl studs
- 4 #60 gold flathead studs
- 16 #60 silver domed square studs
- Custom Hand Tool
- 64 #20 gold pearl studs

Note: Complete one side of the box first, and then repeat the procedure for each remaining side.

1 Place the #60 plunger into the Be-Dazzler machine and turn the setter plate to #20. Insert #60 silver pearl studs along the top and bottom of one side, equally spaced apart.

2 Now insert a #60 gold flathead stud directly in the center of one side; this is the center of the design.

3 Follow the Western Star pattern on page 87 and insert the silver domed square studs with the Custom Hand Tool, four around the gold flathead stud. (**Note:** Do not transfer the pattern with an iron onto the paper.)

4 Now place the #20 plunger into the Be-Dazzler machine and turn the setter plate to #20. Insert #20 gold pearl studs into the shade, following the pattern.

Polarfleece Blanket

Project 43

Curl up in this soft, cozy blanket and chase away the chills! This project is so incredibly quick and easy to make, it would make an ideal gift.

▲▽◄▲▽▲▽◄▲▽◄▲▽◄▲▽◄▲▽◄▲▽◄▲▽◄▲▽◄▲▽◄▲▽◄▲▽◄▲▽◄▲▽◄▲▽

Designed by Elaine Schmidt

You Will Need

- ◎ 65" x 65" piece of polarfleece, green
- ◎ 7-1/2 yards of 1" grosgrain ribbon, red
- ◎ 52 #40 silver flathead studs
- ◎ Ruler or measuring tape
- ◎ Vanishing fabric marker
- ◎ Scissors
- ◎ Fabric glue

Note: Instructions for the floral pillow can be found on page 71. Instructions for the wire-embellished pillow can be found on page 68.

1 Lay the polarfleece on a flat surface. Measure and mark a 4" square on each corner. Cut each corner away.

2 To make the fringe, cut 4" long by 1/2" wide strips into the sides of the blanket; you'll be cutting approximately 80 fringes on each edge of the blanket.

3 To make the ribbon slots, measure in 7-1/2" (including the fringes) on both sides of each corner and cut a 1" long slot.

4 Cut 1" long slots every 4", all of the way around the blanket.

5 Cut four pieces of ribbon, one equal in length to each side of the blanket. Trim a "v" shape out of each ribbon end. Weave the ribbon through the slots on each side of the blanket as shown.

6 Place the #20 plunger into the Be-Dazzler machine and turn the setter plate to #20. Set a stud at the intersection of the ribbons in each corner of the blanket. Use fabric glue to affix the ribbon to the blanket at each corner.

7 Set two studs in each 4" section of ribbon around each side of the blanket.

8 Use the fabric glue to fasten the rest of the ribbon to the blanket (top and bottom).

Wild Wire Pillow

Project 44

Designed by Elaine Schmidt

The addition of wire to this simple design turns the ordinary into something quite extraordinary!

You Will Need

- 2 12" x 12" pieces of polarfleece, red
- 11" x 11" pillow form
- 10 #20 silver pearl studs
- 10 #60 silver flat diamond studs
- Custom Hand Tool
- 12" piece of decorative ribbon, blue
- Thread, blue, and needle
- 22 gauge Wild Wire, Silver
- 22 gauge Wild Wire, Powder Blue
- 10 Wild Wire Glass Beads
- Needle Nose, Round Nose, and Nylon Jaw Pliers
- Wire Cutters
- Sewing machine

Note: Use 1/2" seam allowance.

1 Choose one piece of polarfleece for the pillow front. On this piece, stitch the blue ribbon on, about 4" down from the top edge.

2 Using the Custom Hand Tool, insert the silver flat diamond studs into the polarfleece, just above the ribbon. Space the studs at equal distances.

3 Place the #20 plunger into the Be-Dazzler machine and turn the setter plate to #20. Insert #20 silver pearl studs into the polarfleece, one just above each flat diamond stud.

4 Place the pillow front face up on your work surface. Now set the other piece of polarfleece on top of the pillow front. Stitch around the two pieces, leaving the bottom open for inserting the pillow form in Step 7. Turn the pillow right side out.

5 Using the Silver wire as a core, and the Powder Blue wire as the double coil, follow the instructions on page 18 to create ten double coil beads. Complete each wire bead with one glass bead.

6 Using the blue thread, stitch each completed wire bead onto the ribbon, directly beneath each stud set.

7 Insert the pillow form into the finished pillow.

8 Whipstitch the bottom opening closed.

Single Blossom Pillow

Project 45

So often, one single motif can have quite an impact! Here, one flower outlined with round studs looks fresh and inviting.

▲▼◀▲▼◀▲▼◀▲▼◀▲▼◀▲▼◀▲▼◀▲▼◀▲▼◀▲▼◀▲▼◀▲▼◀▲▼◀▲▼◀▲▼◀▲▼◀▲▼◀

Designed by Elaine Schmidt

You Will Need

- 2 18" x 18" pieces of polarfleece, 1 light blue, 1 dark blue
- 12" x 12" pillow form
- Polarfleece scraps, yellow and red
- 105 #40 silver flathead studs
- 24 #20 silver flathead studs
- Rotary cutter with wavy edge blade and cutting mat
- Scissors
- Fabric glue
- Large Flower pattern

1 Trim the light blue piece of polarfleece to a 15" x 15" square, using the rotary cutter, wavy edge blade, and cutting mat.

2 Using the Large Flower pattern on page 87, cut out the flower from the red polarfleece and the center from yellow.

3 Glue the yellow center onto the flower.

4 Place the #20 plunger into the Be-Dazzler machine and turn the setter plate to #20. Go around the center of the flower with #20 studs.

5 Glue the flower onto the center of the light blue pillow top.

6 Place the #40 plunger into the Be-Dazzler machine and turn the setter plate to #40. Attach the #40 studs around the edges of the flower.

7 For the dark blue pillow bottom, cut a 1" square out of each corner. To make the fringe, cut 1" long by 1/2" wide strips into each edge.

8 Lay the pillow bottom on a flat surface. Place the pillow form directly in the center of the bottom. Place the pillow top over the form.

9 Attach the pillow top to the bottom by applying #40 studs 1" apart, 1" from the top's edge, all around the pillow.

Garden of Blooms Pillow

Project 46

This simple design is reminiscent of the Come Play With Me outfit on pages 26 and 27...

Designed by Elaine Schmidt

You Will Need

- Two 13" x 13" pieces of polarfleece, dark blue
- 12" x 12" square pillow form
- Heart & Flower Stud Pack
- Retro Stud Pack
- Custom Hand Tool
- 3 #40 silver ringlets
- 18 silver triangle studs
- 20 silver flat diamond studs
- 14 #40 silver pearl studs
- 31 #20 silver pearl studs
- Sewing machine
- Thread, blue, and needle

Note: Use 1/2" seam allowance.

1. Choose one piece of polarfleece for the pillow top.

2. You will be creating the flowers on this pillow freehand. For the flowers on the left and right sides, insert one flower stud as the center using the Custom Hand Tool. Surround each center with diamond studs. To create the stems, use #20 studs for the upper sections and then complete each stem with two or three #40 studs. Finally, insert two diamond studs on each side of the stems for leaves with the Custom Hand Tool.

3. To create the larger middle flower, insert one ringlet as the flower center. Surround each center with triangle studs with the Custom Hand Tool, as shown (note that the flower at right uses only three studs while the other two use six). To create the stems, use #20 studs for the upper sections and then complete them with #40 studs. Randomly place the remaining triangle studs along the stems for leaves with the Custom Hand Tool.

4. Using the Custom Hand Tool, insert two butterfly studs into the pillow top.

5. With right sides together, machine stitch three sides of the pillow top and bottom. Turn right side out.

6. Insert the pillow form into the finished pillow.

7. Whipstitch the opening closed.

Regal Red Pillow

Project 47

This fringe-edged pillow has a center panel with a wavy-cut edge that has a modern look.

Designed by Elaine Schmidt

You Will Need

- 2 18" x 18" pieces of polarfleece, red and light blue
- Polarfleece scraps, yellow and green
- 12" x 12" pillow form
- Rotary cutter with wavy edge blade and cutting mat
- Scissors
- 43 #40 silver flathead studs
- 56 #20 silver flathead studs
- Small Flower and Small Leaf patterns

1 Trim the red piece of polarfleece to a 15" x 15" square, using the rotary cutter, wavy edge blade, and cutting mat.

2 Using the Small Flower and Small Leaf patterns from page 88, cut out the flowers from the yellow polarfleece and the leaves from green. Cut out seven of each.

3 Glue the flowers and leaves in any arrangement desired to the red pillow front.

4 Place the #20 plunger into the Be-Dazzler machine and turn the setter plate to #20. Put a line of #20 studs down the length of each leaf.

5 Place the #40 plunger into the Be-Dazzler machine and turn the setter plate to #40. Attach the #40 studs into the center of each flower.

7 For the light blue pillow bottom, cut a 1" square out of each corner. To make the fringe, cut 1" long by 1/2" wide strips into each edge.

8 Lay the pillow bottom on a flat surface. Place the pillow form directly in the center of the bottom. Place the pillow top over the form.

9 Attach the pillow top to the bottom by applying #40 studs 1" apart, 1" from the top's edge, all around the pillow.

Trimmed Table Runner

Project 48

Imagine how elegant you could make any table look with this stunning runner!

Designed by Elaine Schmidt

You Will Need

- Table runner, blue
- 2 premade tassels, blue
- 84 #60 silver domed square studs
- Custom Hand Tool
- 28 #40 silver pearl studs
- 20 gauge Wild Wire, Copper
- 22 gauge Wild Wire, Silver
- Needle Nose, Round Nose, and Nylon Jaw Pliers
- Wire Cutters
- Thread, blue, and needle
- Large Diamond pattern

1 Transfer the Large Diamond pattern on page 88 onto each end of the table runner. Using the Custom Hand Tool, insert the silver domed square studs onto the table runner, following the pattern.

2 Place the #40 plunger into the Be-Dazzler machine and turn the setter plate to #40. Starting at one corner of the runner, insert a #40 silver pearl stud.

3 Now, alternate the silver domed square studs and silver pearl studs, equally spaced, around the entire runner.

4 Using the Silver and Copper wire and following the instructions on page 18, create two coiled wire beads.

5 Slide one bead onto each tassel. Stitch one tassel to each table runner end point.

6 Wrap Silver wire around each tassel numerous times, near the top.

7 Create eight Silver wire spirals as shown on page 19. Attach four spirals to each wrapped tassel.

Purple Placemat Set

Projects
49-50-51

Designed by Elaine Schmidt

You Will Need for Placemat

- Placemat, purple
- 20 #20 silver flathead studs
- 10 #60 silver flathead studs
- 20 silver triangle studs
- Custom Hand Tool

You Will Need for Napkin

- Napkin, purple
- 2 #20 silver flathead studs
- 1 #60 silver flathead stud
- 2 silver triangle studs
- Custom Hand Tool

You Will Need for Napkin Ring

- Napkin ring
- Fabric to match napkin and placemat
- 7 #60 silver flathead studs
- Fabric glue

Placemat

1 Place the #60 plunger into the Be-Dazzler machine and turn the setter plate to #20. Insert silver flathead studs into the placemat, three on each long side and two on each short side, evenly spaced apart, as shown.

2 Using the Custom Hand Tool, insert a silver triangle stud on each side of each #60 silver flathead stud. Have one point of each triangle point away from the flathead stud.

3 Place the #20 plunger into the Be-Dazzler machine and turn the setter plate to #20. Insert #20 silver flathead studs into the placemat, next to the point of each triangle, as shown.

Napkin

1 Place the #60 plunger into the Be-Dazzler machine and turn the setter plate to #20. Insert the silver flathead stud into the napkin, about 2" from one corner.

2 Using the Custom Hand Tool, insert a silver triangle stud on each side of each #60 silver flathead stud. Have one point of each triangle point away from the flathead stud.

3 Place the #20 plunger into the Be-Dazzler machine and turn the setter plate to #20. Insert #20 silver flathead studs into the napkin, next to the point of each triangle, as shown.

Napkin Ring

1 Cut a piece of fabric to fit around napkin ring, plus 1/2".

2 Place the #60 plunger into the Be-Dazzler machine and turn the setter plate to #20. Insert the #60 flathead studs into the fabric, evenly spaced apart.

3 Fold 1/2" at one end back and glue to hold in place. Glue the fabric around the napkin ring, using the folded and glued end to overlap the other end.

Country Stars Placemat Set

This fun denim placemat and napkin ring set has a Western feel that is hard to resist!

Designed by Elaine Schmidt

You Will Need

- Denim placemat
- Denim napkin ring
- 13 silver large star studs
- 26 #40 ringlets

1 For each placemat corner, use the Custom Hand Tool to apply three large star studs.

2 Place the #40 plunger into the Be-Dazzler machine and turn the setter plate to #40. Set five ringlets into each corner as shown.

3 For the napkin ring, use the Custom Hand Tool to apply one large star stud in the center. Place the #40 plunger into the Be-Dazzler machine and turn the setter plate to #40. Set three ringlets on each side of the star.

Festive Tablecloth and Placemat Set

Projects 54-55

Bring a fun, summery feel to your table with this wire-embellished tablecloth and simple placemat and napkin set. You can make a variety of wire beads with single and double coils, as well as simple coils with beads.

▼◀▲▼◀▲▼◀▲▼◀▲▼◀▲▼◀▲▼◀▲▼◀▲▼◀▲▼◀▲▼◀▲▼◀▲▼◀▲▼◀

Designed by Elaine Schmidt

Note: The plates and napkin rings were embellished with Decor It! paint from NSI Innovations. While it is not recommended to paint the area on which you will place food, it can be used on plate rims, as shown.

You Will Need for Tablecloth

- Square tablecloth, red
- 1/4" grosgrain ribbon, orange, in length to go around perimeter of tablecloth
- Pompom trim, blue, in length to go around perimeter of tablecloth
- 56 #20 silver pearl studs
- 56 silver triangle studs
- Custom Hand Tool
- 20 and 22 gauge Wild Wire, in various colors
- Wild Wire Glass Beads
- Needle Nose, Round Nose, and Nylon Jaw Pliers
- Wire Cutters
- Fabric glue

1 About 1-1/2" from the tablecloth edge, attach the orange ribbon using fabric glue, crossing the ribbon in the corners.

2 Using fabric glue, attach the blue pompom trim all around the tablecloth, covering the ends of the orange ribbon at the corners.

3 Using the Custom Hand Tool, evenly space fourteen silver triangle studs along each side of the tablecloth, just above the orange ribbon, with one long edge placed along the ribbon.

4 Place the #20 plunger into the Be-Dazzler machine and turn the setter plate to #20. Insert one #20 silver pearl stud into the tablecloth, above each triangle.

5 Using the Wild Wire, various pliers, and glass beads, make 56 coiled wire beads and "simple coils" with glass beads, as shown on pages 18 and 19.

6 Attach the beads to the blue pompom trim, fourteen coils and beads to each side.

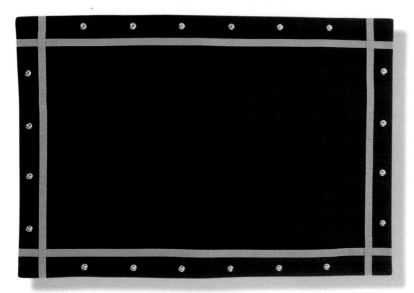

You Will Need for Placemat

- Placemat, blue
- 20 #40 silver pearl studs
- 1/4" grosgrain ribbon, green
- Fabric glue
- Scissors

1 Measure the length and width of the placemat; cut two pieces of ribbon that match the length, adding 2" to each length, and two pieces of ribbon that match the width, adding 2" to each length.

2 Using the fabric glue, attach the ribbons to each placemat about 1-1/2" from each edge, overlapping 1" underneath to the bottom of the placemat.

3 Place the #40 plunger into the Be-Dazzler machine and turn the setter plate to #40. Insert four studs along each short side of the placemat (width); insert six studs along each long side of the placemat (length).

You Will Need for Napkin

- Napkin, red
- 1/4" grosgrain ribbon, orange
- 1 #20 silver pearl stud
- 1 #40 silver pearl stud
- 22 gauge Wild Wire, Dark Blue
- 22 gauge Wild Wire, Silver
- Needle Nose, Round Nose, and Nylon Jaw Pliers
- Wire Cutters
- Thread, red, and needle

1 Measure one side of the napkin; cut two pieces of ribbon that match the length, adding 2".

2 Using the fabric glue, attach the ribbons to two adjacent sides of the napkin about 1" from the edge, overlapping the ribbon 1" underneath to the bottom of the napkin.

3 Place the #40 plunger into the Be-Dazzler machine and turn the setter plate to #40. Insert the #40 silver pearl stud into the napkin, just above the intersection of the ribbon at the corner.

4 Place the #20 plunger into the Be-Dazzler machine and turn the setter plate to #20. Insert the #20 silver pearl stud into the napkin, just above the #40 stud.

5 Following the instructions on page 18, create one double coil wire bead.

6 Attach the completed bead to the corner of the placemat with thread.

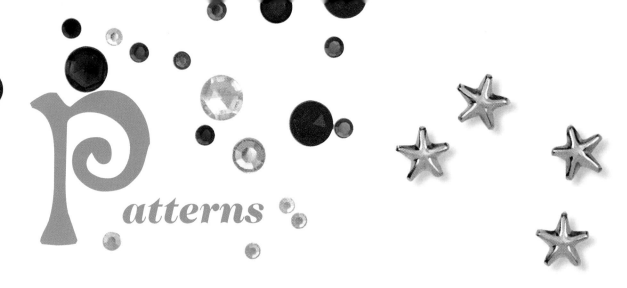

Patterns

So, you've chosen the perfect project to Be-Dazzle, but now you need to design it. Fear not! In this section, we have included full-size patterns that can be transferred onto your project by following the instructions on page 12. Please follow the instructions carefully and always test the hot-iron transfer pencil and iron on an unnoticeable section of you project to ensure satisfactory results! And remember that if you are setting a project solely with rhinestones you need to transfer the pattern onto the wrong side of the fabric. Finally, do not transfer any marks, like centerlines or arrows, onto your project!

As an added bonus, we have included extra patterns that you can use to design your own unique, original fashions, accessories, and home décor items. This is your chance to experiment and have fun!

Note: Some patterns in this section (i.e. the hearts on page 86) are not meant to be transferred onto a project; you will be using such patterns to cut out paper or fabric to be adhered to the project. See individual projects for instructions.

Tips and More!

Read this section to find out more about transferring patterns and how to wash your creations.

Transfers With Studs and Rhinestones

There are some patterns that are designed to be used with both studs and rhinestones. In these cases, transfer the design on the right side of the garment. First, insert all of the studs. Then, use a straight pin to poke through the garment wherever a rhinestone is to be placed. On the reverse side, where the pin is sticking through, mark the spot with a vanishing fabric marker. Finally, use the marks you made with the vanishing fabric marker to guide you when inserting rhinestone settings.

Washing Instructions

Because the transferring method described in this book is permanent, be careful to place your pattern accurately and have sufficient studs and rhinestones to cover the dots! Both before and after washing, check all prongs to make sure studs and rhinestones are securely fastened with prongs flat against the fabric or stone. This is especially important on garments made for children. Turn the garment inside out to avoid damage to the studs and stones as well as the inside of the washer and dryer. Use the gentle cycle or place the garment in a net laundry bag. Wash lightweight or delicate fabrics by hand and hang them to dry. Do not dry clean if you have used acrylic rhinestones.

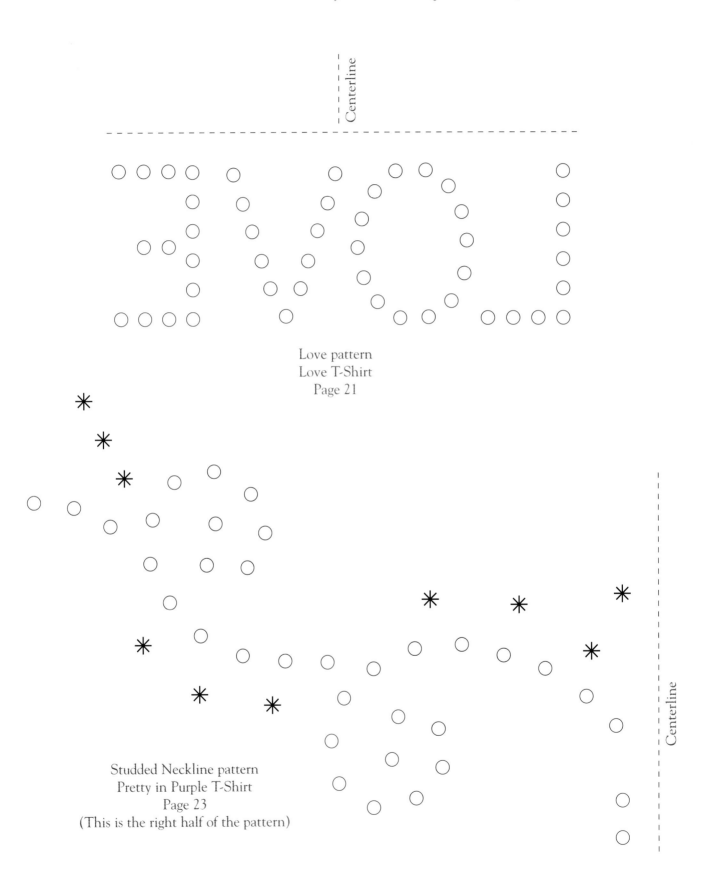

Centerline

Love pattern
Love T-Shirt
Page 21

Studded Neckline pattern
Pretty in Purple T-Shirt
Page 23
(This is the right half of the pattern)

Centerline

Centerline

Studded Neckline pattern
Pretty in Purple T-Shirt
Page 23
(This is the left half of the pattern)

Small Star
Western Denim Shirt
Page 24

Small Boot
Western Denim Shirt
Page 24

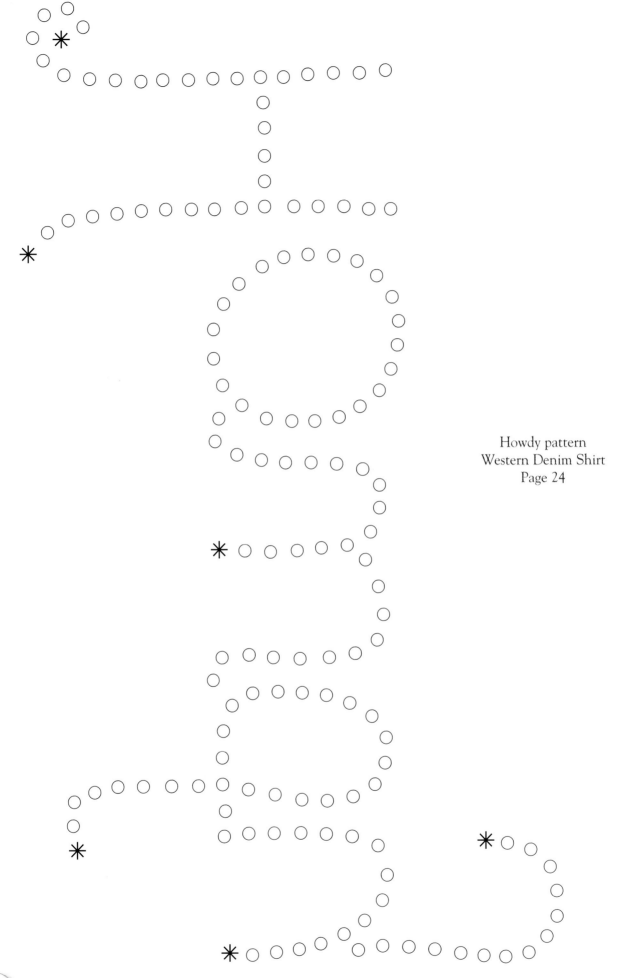

Howdy pattern
Western Denim Shirt
Page 24

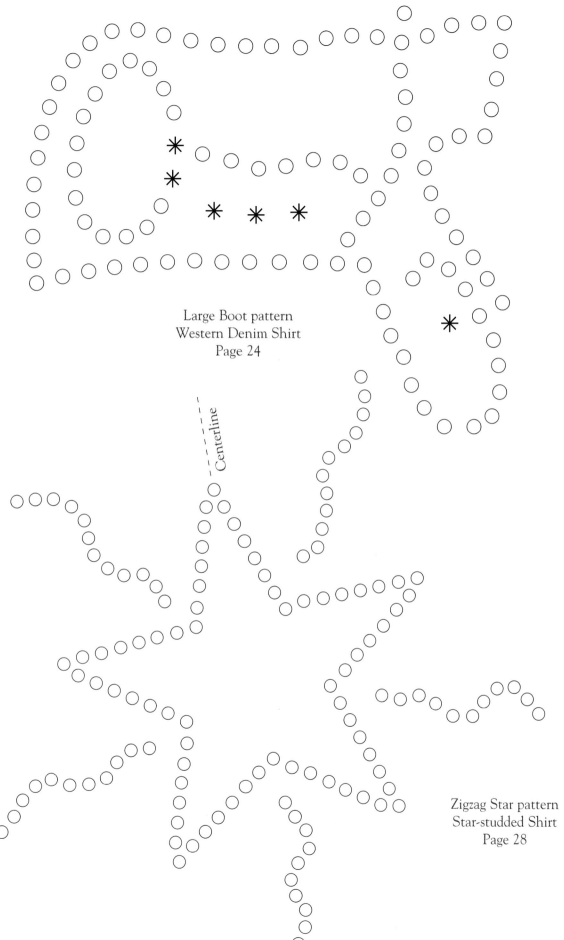

Large Boot pattern
Western Denim Shirt
Page 24

Centerline

Zigzag Star pattern
Star-studded Shirt
Page 28

Swirl 1 pattern
Swirl and Whirl Shirt and Skirt
Page 32
(This is the bottom half for shirt
and entire pattern for skirt)

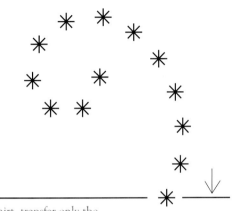

For the shirt, transfer only the
marks below the line (to complete the design). Line up the
arrows with those from the
Swirl 2 pattern.

Do not transfer these
eight stud markings
(to the right) onto the
skirt (see photo on
page 32).

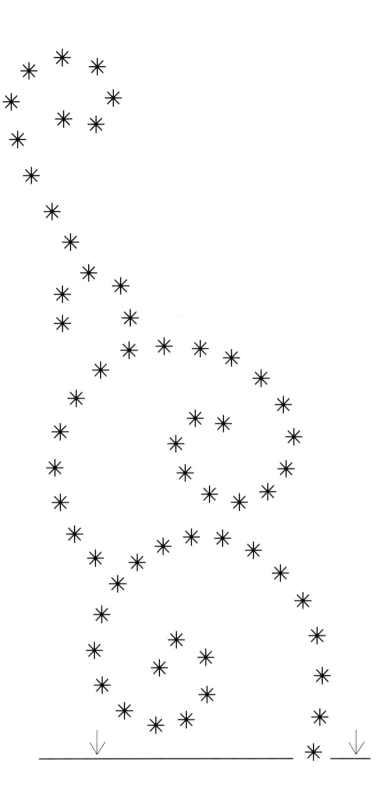

Swirl 2 pattern
Swirl and Whirl Shirt and Skirt
Page 32
(This is the top half for the shirt)

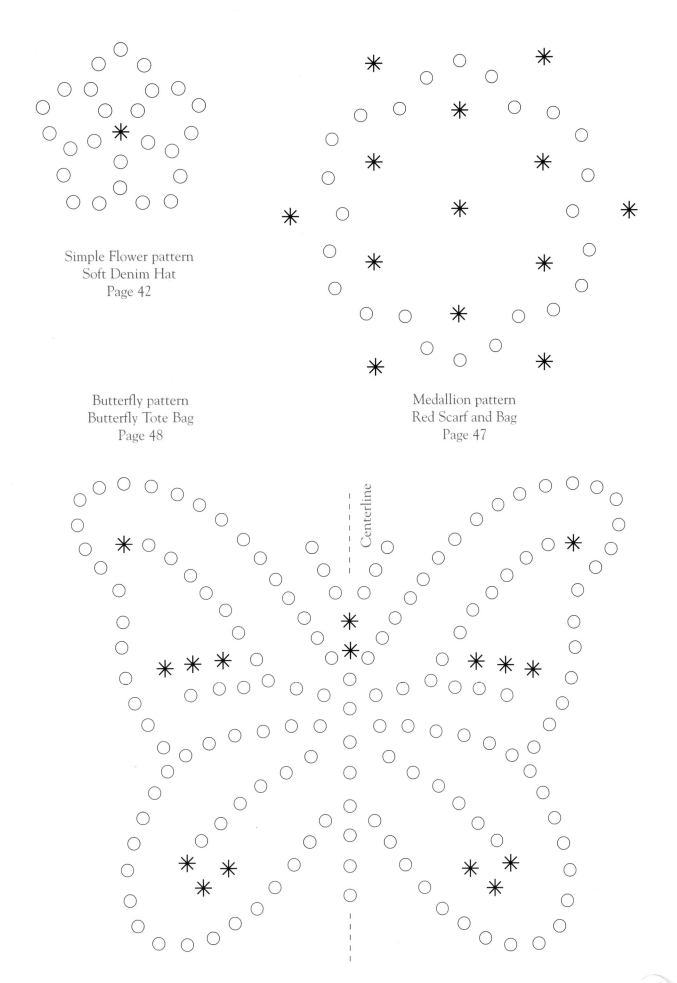

Simple Flower pattern
Soft Denim Hat
Page 42

Butterfly pattern
Butterfly Tote Bag
Page 48

Medallion pattern
Red Scarf and Bag
Page 47

Centerline

Large Heart pattern
Heartfelt Card
Page 56

Small Heart pattern
Heartfelt Card
Page 56

Western Star pattern
Western Lampshade and
Tissue Box Cover
Page 64

Large Flower pattern
Single Blossom Pillow
Page 69

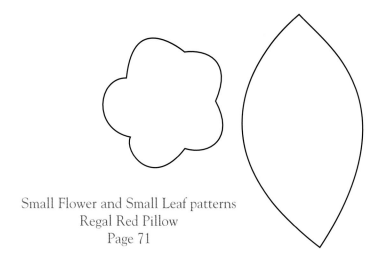

Small Flower and Small Leaf patterns
Regal Red Pillow
Page 71

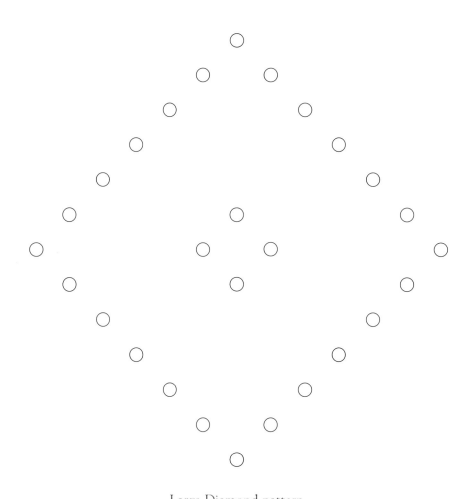

Large Diamond pattern
Trimmed Table Runner
Page 72

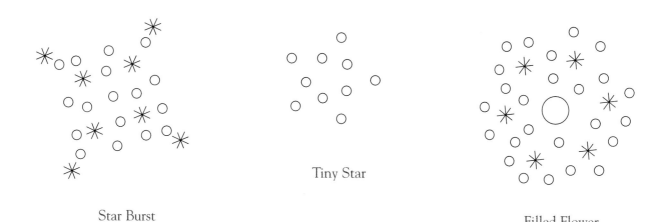

Star Burst

Tiny Star

Filled Flower

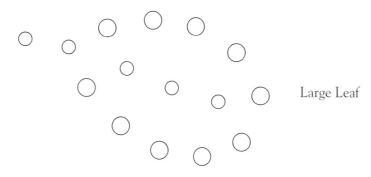

Large Leaf

Zigzag Border

Filled Star

Snowflake

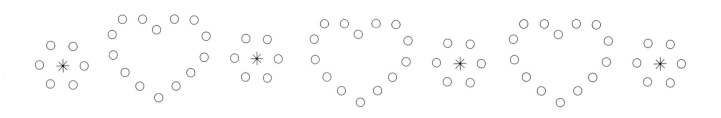

Heart Border

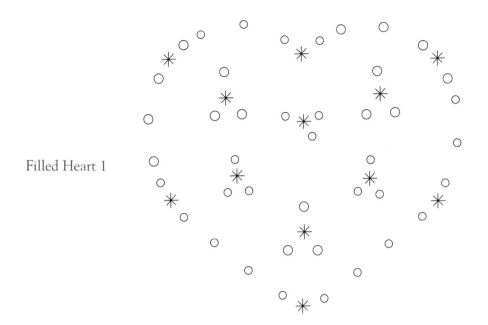

Filled Heart 1

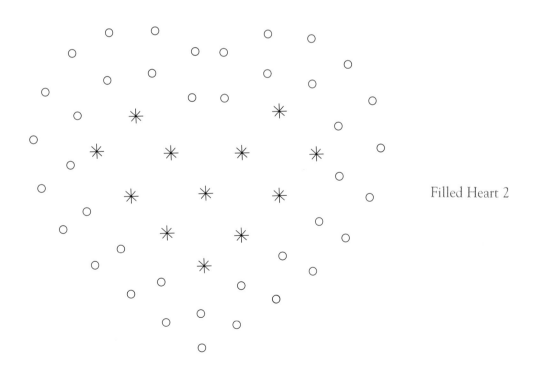

Filled Heart 2

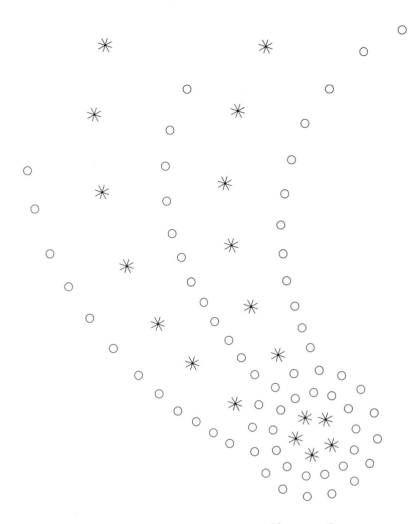

Shooting Star

Mini Swirl

Project Index

Shirts

Project 1:
Love T-shirt
Page 21

Project 2:
Rhinestone T-shirt
Page 22

Project 3:
Pretty in Purple T-shirt
Page 23

Project 4:
Western Denim Shirt
Page 24

Project 5:
Come Play Shirt
Page 26

Project 7:
Star-studded Shirt
Page 28

Project 9:
T-shirt
Page 30

Project 11:
Swirl and Whirl Shirt
Page 32

Jackets

Project 16:
Stars and Stripes
Jean Jacket
Page 38

Project 17:
Trimmed and
Studded Jean Jacket
Page 40

Project 31:
Simple Studded
Jean Jacket
Page 52

Accessories

Project 18:
Straw Hat With
Ribbon Trim
Page 41

Project 19:
Soft Denim Hat
Page 42

Project 20:
Studded Headband
Page 43

Projects 21, 22, and 23:
Punky Belt, Choker,
and Cuffs
Page 44

Project 24:
Snowflakes and
Stars Shawl
Page 46

Projects 25 and 26:
Red Scarf and Bag
Page 47

Project 27:
Butterfly Tote Bag
Page 48

Project 28:
Beaded, Fringed Bag
Page 49

Project 29:
Fun Fringed Shoes
Page 50

Project 30:
Easy Tie
Page 51

Jeans, Pants, and Skirts

Project 6:
Come Play Capris
Page 26

Project 8:
Star-studded Bell
Bottoms
Page 28

Project 10:
Beaded, Fringed Capri
Jeans
Page 30

Project 11:
Swirl and Whirl Skirt
Page 32

Project 13:
Studded Jeans
Page 34

Project 14:
Pink Fringed Jeans
Page 35

Project 15:
Flower Power Jeans
Page 36

Home Decor

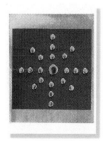

Project 32:
"Denim" Card
Page 55

Project 33:
Heartfelt Card
Page 56

Project 34:
Smile Card
Page 57

Project 35:
Vintage Photo Frame
Page 58